DEVELOPMENT AID TO NEPAL

NORDIC INSTITUTE OF ASIAN STUDIES
Recent NIAS Reports

Development Aid to Nepal

Issues and Options in Energy, Health, Education, Democracy and Human Rights

Harald O. Skar
Sven Cederroth

NIAS

CURZON

Nordic Institute of Asian Studies
NIAS Report Series, No. 34

First published in 1997 by

Nordic Institute of Asian Studies (NIAS)
Leifsgade 33, 2300 Copenhagen S, Denmark
ISBN 87-87062-61-5
ISSN 0904-597x

Curzon Press
15 The Quadrant, Richmond,
Surrey TW9 1BP
ISBN 0-7007-1037-X

British Library Catalogue in Publication Data
A CIP catalogue record for this book
is available from the British Library

About the Authors

Harald O. Skar is director of research at the Norwegian Institute of
International Affairs (NUPI) in Oslo. Sven Cederroth is a research
fellow at the Nordic Institute of Asian Studies in Copenhagen.

Contents

LIST OF TABLES

LIST OF FIGURES

Preface

At the end of August 1996, the Nordic Institute of Asian Studies (NIAS) was commissioned by the Norwegian Foreign Ministry to undertake a study entitled 'Development Aid to Nepal: A Summary of Experiences' (Bistands-erfaringer i Nepal: Mandat for Erfaringsoppsummering). It was expected that this study should be carried out with an input of two researcher-months. The authors were contracted to carry out this work for one month each.

In order to complete the study, printed material in the form of project reports, evaluations and articles from scientific journals and books relating to the issues discussed had to be compiled. We are grateful for the assistance of NIAS librarian Eva Nielsen in identifying relevant data bases and making sure that the material arrived within the short time available. In the course of the study Harald O. Skar undertook an eight-day visit to Nepal where he met with and interviewed people from various bilateral and multilateral development organisations as well as ministers and staff from the concerned line ministries of the Nepalese government. While in Nepal, he worked with Hilde Harket, a project assistant from the Norwegian Institute of International Affairs, and educational consultant Halvard Kulöy of the International Movement towards Educational Change

(IMTEC). Meanwhile, Sven Cederroth compiled material and conducted interviews in Norway, mainly concerning experiences of Norwegian assistance in the energy sector. In this, he was assisted by Laila Tingvold to whom a special word of thanks is due.

Finally, we wish to thank our Nepalese co-ordinator, Dr Ganesh Mar Gurung, for his support during the eight days of hectic data collection in Nepal. Without his help, we would never have gained access to so many ministries (eight in all) and as many high officials and political celebrities as we did. We also thank his colleague, Mr. Bhuva Dahal, for the translation of many Nepalese documents, including the "Resource Book" (see page 9 below), and at NIAS special thanks go to Liz Bramsen who keyed the series of tables based on this and to Gerald Jackson who reworked the report into its current form.

The present study is largely the same as the report submitted to the Norwegian Foreign Ministry in October 1996. However, it has been polished by a substantial editing and the addition of some explanatory material.

The study begins with a short overview that covers the political, economical and social situation in Nepal, focusing especially on factors that are of importance for the planning and initiation of development activities. The total development aid to Nepal from 1990 onwards, analysed by donor and sector, is reported in tabular form. The study focuses on experiences of development aid in four sectors: health, education, energy and democracy/human rights. For each of these four sectors, the Nepalese development strategy and experiences of Norwegian organisations who have been working in Nepal are discussed. Different channels for Norwegian aid, including that via private organisations, are also evaluated. The formal, as well as the actual role of the civil service is described as is Nepal's capacity to absorb aid in these four sectors. Finally, gender and environmental aspects are considered.

In the draft report submitted we attempted to meet the requirements in the terms of reference to the highest degree possible. We were not able, however, to go into details of such private organisations as the Norwegian NGOs working in Nepal. We suggest that a separate review should be carried out on all the NGOs, local, international and Norwegian. Indeed, special attention focused on the largest international NGO in Nepal, the United Mission to Nepal, could well provide interesting data.

However, one of the requirements in the terms of reference was that the volume of aid be provided in tabular form. It proved to be an impossible task to obtain this information, even from the Ministry of Finance in Nepal. However, we have compensated for this omission by making the first ever translation into English of the Nepalese document popularly termed the "Resource Book". Used by the Nepalese Ministry of Finance, this is a total review of "who is doing what" with regard to foreign aid in Nepal for the fiscal year 1996–97. We are proud to be able to present this document in tabular form (see Appendix 2). Also included in the appendices is a Norwegian resume of the study.

Harald O. Skar   Sven Cederroth

List of Abbreviations

ADB	Asian Development Bank
BEC	Butwal Engineering Company
BPC	Butwal Power Company
BTI	Butwal Technical Institute
CARE	Cooperative for Assistance and Relief Everywhere
CIDA	Canadian International Development Agency
CPN-UML	Communist Party of Nepal
DANIDA	Danish International Development Assistance
DDC	District Development Committee
EDC	Electric Development Centre
GW	gigawatt (1,000 megawatts)
HH	Himal Hydro (company)
HMG	His Majesty's Government (the government of Nepal)
IIMI	International Irrigation Management Institute
IMTEC	International Movement towards Educational Change
INSEC	Informal Services Centre
MW	megawatt
MWR	Ministry of Water Resources
NCP	Nepali Congress Party
NDP	National Democratic Party
NEA	Nepal Electricity Authority
NGO	non-governmental organisation

NHE	Nepal Hydro and Electric
NIAS	Nordic Institute of Asian Studies
NORAD	Norwegian Agency for Development Cooperation
NPC	National Planning Commission
NVE	Norges Vassdrags- og Energiverk
ODA	Official Development Assistance
SA	Statkraft Anlegg (company)
SDP	Nepal Sadhbhavana Party
SE	Statkraft Engineering (company)
UMN	United Mission to Nepal
VDC	Village Development Committee

Figure 1: Map of Nepal

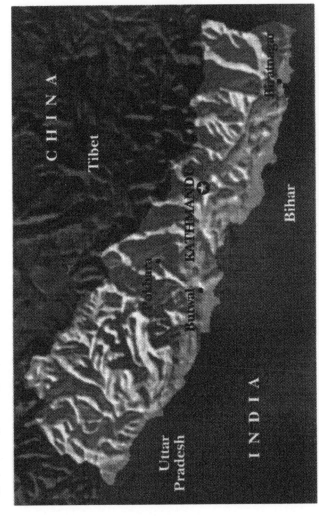

Nepal: A Brief Overview

POLITICAL, ECONOMIC AND SOCIAL SITUATION

The Population

In mid-1993 it was estimated that Nepal had a population of 19.3 million people. Nepal is ethnically diverse and complex with more than 75 ethnic groups speaking some 50 languages.

Broadly speaking, the population can be classified into three major ethnic groupings based on origin: Indo-Nepalese, Tibeto-Mongols and indigenous Nepalese. Coming into the country as they did from different directions, the two first groups are today found in different parts of the country at various altitudes. The Indo-Nepalese inhabit the Terai, the river valleys and the fertile lower hills while the Tibeto-Mongols (who have much in common with the Tibetans) occupy the higher northern mountain areas from west to east. In the central hill region there are many different groups of people among whom the Brahmans (13 per cent), the Chettris (16 per cent) and the Newars (5.6 per cent) are dominant. Generally speaking, the Indo-Nepalese peoples have been agriculturists while the Tibeto-Mongol groups can be considered agro-pastoralists, the emphasis on agriculture versus pastoralism shifting depending on the local environment. The third group, the indigenous Nepalese, consists of a number of tribal communities such as the Tharus and the Dhimals living in the Terai. Culturally and linguistically, these people are closely related to people in the north Indian states of Uttar Pradesh and Bihar.

Even though the Indo-Nepalese arrived later than the Tibeto-Mongols, they have come to dominate the country, socially, politically and economically. This group, most of whom fled to Nepal in the wake of Muslim invasions of northern India several hundred years ago, was largely of high-caste (Brahman and Kshatriya) Hindu origin. The Indo-Nepalese have since spread throughout much of the country and now comprise more than 50 per cent of the total population. They have a dominant role, being large landowners and constituting a significant portion of the national and local elites (including the royal family itself). In 1991, 80 per cent of the posts in the civil service, army and police were held by the Brahmans and Chhetris of the hills.

Brahmans and Chettries also dominate within the two main political parties (see page 15 below), often rationalising their caste interests as national interests. Ethnic-based political parties are not allowed according to the 1990 constitution since such "may jeopardize the harmonious relations subsisting among the peoples of various castes, tribes or communities". According to the constitution each community "shall have the right to preserve and promote its language, script and culture". Each community also has the right to have schools operating in its mother tongue up to the end of the primary level.

Nepalese Politics in the 1990s

Until 1990, recent Nepalese politics operated within the confines of the non-party *panchayat* system based on an

absolute monarchy. Introduced in 1962, this system prohibited political parties and operated largely under the
guidance of the palace. Popular dissatisfaction with the
panchayat system was fuelled by a year-long Indian economic blockade in 1989. Huge demonstrations staged
by a Movement for the Restoration of Democracy (led by
the Nepali Congress and the United Left Front) brought
about the system's downfall in April 1990.

A new interim government was installed with a
mandate to prepare a new constitution and hold multi-
party elections. These were held a year later and were
won by the Nepali Congress (NCP) with the Communist
Party of Nepal (United Marxist-Leninist) – commonly
known as the UML – as the strongest opposition party.
As a result mainly of internal conflicts and power
struggles, Prime Minister Koirala was forced to resign in
July 1994 and new elections took place on November
15. The UML emerged from this election as the largest
party with 88 out of 205 parliament seats, the NCP
second with 83 seats. Since the UML did not have a
majority it was forced to negotiate with other parties to
form a coalition government. However, when these
negotiations failed, the UML formed a minority government that lasted little more than half a year before it
was brought down by an opposition-initiated "no confidence" motion. Subsequently, a Congress-led coalition
government was formed that included the National
Democratic Party (NDP), a royalist right-of-centre party,
and the Nepal Sadhbhavana Party (SDP), a regional party
mainly supported by Hindu immigrants (see Figure 17
on "Balance of power in the current Nepali parliament"
on page 125). The coalition parties have since issued a
joint policy statement that includes a commitment to
multi-party democracy and adherence to market-oriented
and competitive economic and fiscal policies.

According to the constitution of 1990, Nepal is a "multiethnic" and "multilingual" country where sovereignty is vested in the people. The king no longer has absolute power but is a constitutional monarch whose acts must be approved by the Council of Ministers. Political parties face no restrictions in their work provided that their constitutions are democratic and that they do not limit membership on the basis of religion, community, caste or region. The Communist Party seems to be best organised of the three dominant political parties although there are tensions within the party about the correct political line to be followed. The Nepali Congress lost the 1994 elections mainly due to factional strife within the party between three competing leaders. Finally, the NDP has its base among old *panchayat* politicians and won many votes because of popular displeasure with the feuding NC leadership. The party has a relatively weak organisational base but many ambitious personalities.

Ever since the fall of the Rana regime in 1950 there have been organised peasant movements directed against the regime and those remnants of the feudal system still found in the rural areas. During the *panchayat* period there were many serious uprisings, the most important one being the communist rebellion in eastern Nepal from 1970–73. Peasant movements and the communists are closely interdependent in Nepal. If the present regime fails to satisfy the demands of the peasants and the landless, it may well be that armed rebellion will again grow and eventually become a serious threat to the regime.

The Economy

The Nepalese economy is to a large extent agriculturally based. Some 90 per cent of the population live in the rural areas, but it is only in the southern Terai plain and in a number of valleys in the central hill belt that intensive cultivation takes place. This area covers 21 per cent of the total land area, but has 70 per cent of the total cultivated land and contributes 55 per cent of the agricultural production. In the northern mountainous region less than one per cent of the land is under cultivation. The contribution of agriculture to GDP has continually shrunk during the last 20 years, from 72 per cent in 1974–75 to about 50 per cent in the mid-1980s and 42 per cent in 1994–95.

About 80 per cent of the manufacturing sector is dominated by carpet and garment production. This sector has been rapidly growing in recent years but is still small – in 1993–94 earnings from the sector contributed around 9 per cent of GDP. The exports from carpets and garments alone accounted for 55 per cent of total exports in 1992–93.

During the past decade, the population has grown at an average rate of 2.7 per cent per year. 43 per cent of the population lives below the poverty line and is affected by nutritional deficiency. While the top 10 per cent of households earn 47 per cent of the total income, the bottom 20 per cent earn only 4.6 per cent. Generally speaking, incomes are higher in the central region of the country, including Kathmandu Valley, while the poorest communities are found in the west. During the last five years, wage rates have more or less kept the same pace as inflation.

To sum up, one can say that there has been very limited economic development during the whole period that has been covered by successive five-year development plans from 1956–90. The period has been marked by low GDP and high population growth rates which have led to only marginal improvement in the per

capita income of the people. In 1992 the GNP per
capita was 170 dollars, a rate that was the fifth-lowest in
the world. However, recently there has been signs of
improvement. During the years 1990–91 to 1993–94
there was an average growth rate of 5 per cent; in 1994–
95 it was 7.8 per cent, the highest in South Asia.
Simultaneously, inflation came down from 21 per cent
to less than 10 per cent.

Education

It is the aim of the government to make primary education free for all by the year 2000 and already today it is
free for much of the population. During the 10-year
period from 1983 to 1993 the number of primary school
students almost doubled, rising from 1.6 million to 3.1
million. In 1990, 82 per cent of children attended
primary school (compared to 20 per cent in 1965) but
while virtually all boys went to school only 47 per cent
of girls did so. As for secondary education, close to one
third of those who could attend did so (compared to 5
per cent in 1965) but again the number of boys was
almost double that of girls. In 1993–94 the number of
students enrolled in higher education was 189,000. As a
result of the expanding primary education, the literacy
rate rose from 13 per cent in 1970 to 27 per cent in
1992, but again women lagged behind with only a 14
per cent literacy rate.

Health

Health facilities have also expanded gradually, but still
basic health services are very limited. This is reflected
in a high infant mortality of 107 per 1,000 live births
and a low life expectancy (in 1992 this was 53 years).
There is only one doctor for every 16,829 people and
one hospital bed for every 4,000. In the early 1980s a

plan was introduced with the aim of developing basic health services at the village level over a 15-year perspective. Regional health directorates were established to inspect, supervise and implement the programme. While this scheme is not actually operating, plans for its implementation are still in place. According to the government's basic needs approach, services shall be provided in areas such as treatment of common diseases, safe water supply, sanitation, nutrition, control of epidemic diseases, immunisation, maternal and child health care and family planning.

Energy and Natural Resources

Nepal has the shape of a sloping oblong with an average width of 176 km and an east–west extension of 885 km. Topographically the country is very varied, ranging from the Terai plains with smaller hills up to about 1,200 meters high, followed by a succession of mountains in the central region up to some 3,000 meters and, finally, in the north the Himalayan mountain range (including Mount Everest, the world's highest mountain peak, reaching 8,882 meters high). Despite its small width, the country covers no less than five climatic zones as a result of this topographical variation: tropical, mesothermal, micro-thermal, taiga and tundra.

The most serious environmental problem has to do with overexploitation of forest resources, leading to deforestation and soil erosion. The growing population pressure together with widespread poverty has led to a quick degradation of this limited natural resource. As the scope for internal migration from the mountain areas to the plains of Terai diminishes, more and more of the marginal land is claimed for agricultural purposes and leads to pressure on the vulnerable land on the more or less steep slopes. Firewood is the main source of energy and amounts to more than three quarters (76 per cent) of the total energy consumption. The government is aware of the problems and is attempting to strengthen the institutional framework for environmental protection.

Nepal has vast hydroelectric resources and it has been estimated that the theoretical potential amounts to 83,000 MW, of which 50 per cent can be utilised commercially. Although at present only a very small amount of the potential production is utilised, hydroelectricity is the most important natural resource that Nepal can exploit commercially. The export market is, however, monopolised by Nepal's southern neighbour, India, which tends to dictate prices and thus limit the potential for exports.

The country has known and exploitable mineral reserves consisting of lead, zinc, iron ore, limestone, marble, magnesium and oil. Investigation of exploitation possibilities have been made and investment has begun at a slow but gathering pace.

Gender Perspectives

In 1951 women and men were granted equal political rights, in 1963 the civil code abolished all discrimination against women and finally in 1976 equal pay legislation was enacted. However, despite such legal measures, an analysis of women's status in Nepal reveals many discrepancies between the social and economic well-being of men and women. Legalised discrimination against women is found in the unequal inheritance rights and in the citizenship rights according to which a Nepalese woman who marries a foreigner loses her residence rights. Parliament is presently discussing a bill on female ownership of land, but this is expected to be opposed by the Nepalese Congress and Royalist parties.

An indication of the degree of discrimination is to be found in the fact that Nepal is one of only three countries in the world where women have a lower life expectancy compared to men, 53.4 versus 55.9 years. Only 22 per cent of girls complete primary school and there is a higher percentage of illiterates among women as compared with men. Despite the fact that a higher percentage of women than men are engaged in agricultural and related activities, they receive lower wages than men and, generally speaking, have worse working conditions.

From a cultural point of view, marriage and the begetting of children, especially boys, are the ultimate goals for every woman. Almost 90 per cent of all women are married before they reach the age of 25 and, while the mean age of marriage is now 18 years (a decade ago it was 17 years), still more than 8 per cent of women are married before they reach the age of 15 years. Most marriages are arranged by parents and once married the women have little opportunity to make any independent choices about how they want to live their lives. Therefore, the mean age of marriage is an important social indicator of women's status.

Human Rights and Democracy

Democracy was restored after a primarily urban-based popular movement had forced the king to abandon the *panchayat* system. Since then, three national elections have been held: two parliamentary and one for local government. It seems that, by and large, these elections have been free and fair. Government has changed hands twice, in November 1994 and in September 1995, and both transfers of power have been peaceful. On the whole it can be concluded that, since political reforms began in 1990, Nepal has made considerable progress towards a more open society with greater respect for human rights.

However, problems remain mainly because the government has failed to enforce all provisions of the constitution. It has been alleged that arbitrary arrests and detention occur and that the police commonly uses physical abuse to extract confessions while the government has deferred from investigating allegations about such police brutality. Detainees are often held longer than is permitted by law. Prison conditions are extremely poor and overcrowding is a common phenomenon. There are still some restrictions on freedom of religion and expression. As discussed above, women suffer widespread discrimination and also the trafficking in women and girls remains a serious problem.

The old caste law "Muluki Ain" of 1854 is still in operation in Nepal. It regulates the relationships between all segments of society and endorses the view of Nepal as the only constitutional Hindu country in the world (in opposition to the Buddhist Kingdom of Bhutan). After several amendments the Muluki Ain now prohibits slavery. However, no system of legal jurisdiction or penalty is in operation and thus no legal processing or even sentencing of offenders can take place. Legally, the various international conventions signed by Nepal are the most binding instruments in many court cases and, accordingly, the activities of many Human Rights organisations are based on these.

The judicial system has three levels: district courts, appellate courts and the Supreme Court. The judiciary is fairly independent at the level of Supreme Court, but is vulnerable to political pressures and bribery at lower levels. According to the constitution, there is to be freedom of expression and censorship of news and other reading material is prohibited. However, the constitution also prohibits speech and writing which threatens the sovereignty of the kingdom, disturbs harmonious relations among people of different castes or communities, instigates crime or contradicts decent public behaviour and morality.

The Civil Service

Since the fall of the *panchayat* regime, the new Nepalese constitution has prescribed that executive powers are exercised by the King acting on advice from the Council of Ministers. This council consists of the Prime Minister (appointed by the King but dependent on the command of a parliamentary majority) plus the Deputy Prime Minister and other ministers (appointed by the King upon the recommendation by the Prime Minister). In 1992 the council, known as His Majesty's Government (HMG), controlled 23 ministries and 45 departments but today they have mushroomed and Nepal now has 47 ministries. All of this central administration is located in Kathmandu.

Additionally, there is a structure of local administration which is organised at three levels: region, district and town or village. The country is divided into five regions and 75 districts. In the regions, those ministries con-cerned with development have set up regional offices and in the districts there are district offices concerned primarily with policy implementation and direct contact with the public. Also at village and town level, offices are set up for such purposes as agriculture, health and postal services where district offices alone are not sufficient. There are also elected bodies of local government at district, town and village levels respect-ively. In the 75 districts these are known as a District Develop-ment Committee (DDC) and at village level as a Village Development Committee (VDC). There are

3,995 VDCs in the country and an additional 39 municipalities.

According to the Nepal Civil Service Act of 1956 there are two categories of civil servants, gazetted and non-gazetted. The former category includes all positions for which all vacancies and appointments are advertised in the government gazette, the *Nepal Raj Patra*. In 1991 such positions were found among others in the educational, judicial, health, administrative, engineering, forestry and agricultural services. There has been a tremendous growth in the number of civil servants – numbers have more than doubled during the past 20 years, almost reaching 100,000 in 1991. Most civil servants are drawn from the upper castes in the hills and among the elite population of the Kathmandu valley with comparatively few from the Terai. Patronage rather than competence has always been the most important means of securing posts and achieving promotion in the civil service.

While 84 per cent of Nepal's population lives in rural areas and is agriculturally based, all government offices and the bulk of administration are found in Kathmandu. The Nepalese administration is highly centralised but, although the structure of local government as seen in DDCs, VDCs and municipalities is in accordance with this centralised ideal, in fact the local government system is beset with problems and does not function properly. Generally speaking, the elected local bodies have a weak organisational structure and they never formulate annual and periodic plans the way they are supposed to do because their members lack the planning skills and experience to do this. Funds are often misused and projects financed by DDC grants at VDC level often remain incomplete or are not properly maintained. Recognising and attempting to address these problems, the former UML government introduced a programme called Build

Your Village Yourselves (BOVO) in which each village received a grant of Rs 300,000 to spend through their VDC under the guidance of All Party Advisory Committees. The present government has introduced a Village Development and Self Reliance Programme which has increased the grant to Rs 500,000 but otherwise this is a continuation of BOVO.

Causes of Poverty

The basic cause of poverty can be seen as a combination of a rapid population increase with an insufficient economic base. Nepal has many natural disadvantages such as its landlocked location and difficult terrain. Together with the poor infrastructure, an unskilled work force, a weak managerial capacity and stagnant agricultural output, these combine to create a weak economic base. About one third of the population lives in areas that are inaccessible by road. In these areas input costs are enormously expensive and the possibilities for marketing an agricultural surplus are very limited. Also the costs of constructing roads in the hilly and mountainous terrain are so high that generally it is not feasible.

That Nepal is landlocked results in problems for its exports due to high transport costs and higher border prices for imported intermediate goods. Macro-economically, the main drawback is to be found in Nepal's relations with India. The country is locked behind India's highly protectionist trade barriers and this means that the rate of return on imported third-country goods is high and relatively risk free due to the lack of competition, thus providing few incentives for productive entrepreneurial enterprises. Furthermore, were Nepal to attempt to liberalise its economy, disregarding India's protective barriers, this would result in large-scale smuggling. Therefore, Nepal's range of choices is extremely limited and this situation leads to a slow economic growth which particularly affects the employment opportunities of the poor.

The net cultivated area is only 18 per cent of the total land area and there is very limited scope for expansion. While food-grain production increased by 20 per cent between 1975–88, the population increased twice as fast leading to a situation whereby Nepal, instead of being able to export food, is now a net importer. With an annual population growth of 2.7 per cent, the country has now reached a population density of about 6.2 inhabitants per hectare of cultivated land. Similar densities are found in the fertile Asian deltas but in Nepal they occur mostly on dry lands of mediocre quality. Over the last two generations the density per unit of agricultural land has increased by nearly two and a half times and the availability of agricultural land has declined from 0.6 hectares per person in 1954 to 0.24 in 1990. This has resulted in increasing pressure on poorer agricultural land which in its turn has resulted in soil depletion, forest depletion and erosion.

As a result of the combination of the above factors, the economy has remained almost stagnant over the last 20 years. On average there has been a 3.4-per-cent annual growth but, due to the rapid population increase, the per capita GDP growth has stopped at a yearly rate of 0.7 per cent. Above all it is failure in the agricultural sector that has contributed to this depressing situation. In contrast, manufacturing has grown rapidly, almost 6 per cent per year during the last decade, but it still accounts for only 6 per cent of GDP and 2 per cent of employment, and therefore its effect on economic growth has been limited. The failure to achieve any significant expansion in agriculture especially affects the poor since their income depends on their own production capability and/or on their ability to find employment on the farms of others.

Table 1: Official development assistance to Nepal in 1995 (USD millions)

Bilateral Donors		Multilateral Donors		Sector	
Japan	91.8	ODA	81.6	Transport	69.4
United Kingdom	27.0	ADB	69.8	Agric, Forestry and Fisheries	55.1
USA	22.1	WFP	9.0	Human Resrce Development	39.4
Denmark	21.3	UNICEF	7.3	Humanitarian Aid and Relief	36.7
Germany	14.5	IMF	6.3	Natural Resrces	34.4
Switz'land	13.8	UNDP	5.2	Energy	30.0
Netherl'ds	6.4	UNHCR	4.6	Communication	29.4
Finland	5.5	UNFPA	3.4	Health	27.1
Australia	5.4	EU	2.8	Area Developmt	24.1
Canada	4.5	WHO	1.6	Economic Mgmt	21.2

Development Assistance to Nepal

During 1995, the last year for which statistics are available, the official development assistance to Nepal amounted to a total of USD 430.4 million, a decrease from USD 476.2 million the previous year. Of the external development assistance, 63.4 per cent consisted of grants and the remaining 36.6 per cent were loans. Of the total official development assistance, 50.7 per cent came from bilateral donors, 45.2 per cent from multilateral sources and 4.1 per cent from international NGOs. Among the multilateral donors, the British Overseas Development Agency (ODA) was the largest, contributing 19 per cent of the total official develop-

Table 2: Aid disbursements in the period 1990–91 to 1994–95 (in Rs Million)

Source of aid	90–91	91–92	92–93	93–94	94–95
Bilateral	2939.9	3597.3	3638.5	2627.1	5050.2
Multilateral	3050.1	4203.1	5597.1	8930.1	7260.7
Total	5990.0	7800.4	9235.6	11557.2	12310.9

ment assistance, with the Asian Development Bank (ADB) in second place with a contribution of 16.2 per cent. Among the bilateral donors, Japan was dominant with a contribution of USD 91.8 million with the United Kingdom second, contributing USD 27.0 million. Denmark was the fourth largest bilateral donor with USD 21.3 million. Among the international NGOs, PLAN Inter-

Table 3: Distribution by sector of aid in the period 1990–91 to 1994–95 (in Rs Million)

Sector	90–91	91–92	92–93	93–94	94–95
Agriculture	609.6	396.8	724.9	2,064.9	1,302.4
Irrigation	435.3	1,158.9	1,027.1	1,713.7	1,883.1
Forestry	207.8	389.7	171.2	1,329.8	180.9
Transport	1,357.4	1,128.2	1,466.0	2,119.8	2,861.1
Power	1,163.6	1,243.4	2,008.5	1,632.3	1,253.4
Communic'n	54.6	113.5	465.1	417.3	1,521.8
Education	122.2	205.1	712.3	617.1	1,318.8
Health	105.4	182.0	266.3	226.8	416.2
Drink'g water	181.9	633.0	1,201.6	324.5	374.2
Total	4,237.8	5,450.6	8,043.0	10,446.2	11,111.9

Table 4: Foreign aid disbursement by donor (in Rs millions)

Donor	pre plan pre-1956	1st plan 1956-61	gap year 1961	2nd plan 1962-65	3rd plan 1965-70	4th plan 1970-75	5th plan 1975-80	6th plan 1980-85	TOTAL
China	–	32.1	14.8	45.0	153.1	213.2	307.7	477.4	1,243.3
India	70.0	82.1	40.9	110.0	551.1	569.1	643.6	1,082.5	3,149.4
Soviet Union	–	8.5	44.2	76.8	18.8	7.8	–	–	156.1
United Kingdom	–	3.7	1.6	8.1	13.7	146.1	438.9	501.0	1,113.1
United States	25.0	222.4	82.5	212.7	219.9	211.5	281.2	599.8	1,855.0
Others	–	34.1	2.4	23.4	11.3	112.3	872.1	2,193.6	3,249.2
Total Bilateral	95.0	328.9	186.4	476.0	967.9	1,260.1	2,543.5	4,854.3	10,766.1
Multilateral	–	–	–	–	–	249.0	1,697.3	5,730.9	7,677.2
Grand Total	95.0	382.9	186.4	476.0	967.9	1,509.1	4,240.8	10,585.2	18,443.3

national was the largest contributor, disbursing USD 4.1 million, the United Mission to Nepal (UMN) was second with USD 3.2 million and CARE was third, disbursing USD 2.3 million. The contribution in 1995 of major multilateral and bilateral donors as well as distribution by sector can be seen in Table 1 (see page 27 above). During the five-year period immediately preceding, the aid disbursements from bilateral and multilateral donors respectively and distribution by sector have been reported as seen in Table 2 (see page 28 above.) How this was disbursed by sector is shown in Table 3 (see page 28 above). Finally, the pattern of aid disbursement by donor in the period prior to 1985 is shown in Table 4 (see page 29 above). This is analysed by sector in Table 5 (below).

Table 5: Allocation of foreign aid by sector (per cent)

Sector	Pre-4th Plan*	4th Plan	5th Plan	6th Plan	Total
Transport & comms	39.10	38.60	38.16	19.46	26.95
Industry and power	17.24	22.80	28.32	30.28	27.92
Agriculture	19.61	19.50	19.33	30.07	25.89
Social services	16.16	14.90	13.74	19.00	17.27
Others	7.79	4.20	0.45	1.19	1.98

*Note: period 1951–52 to end of 3rd Plan.

Energy Development

THE NEPALESE ENERGY SECTOR

At present Nepalese energy consumption is heavily dependent on biomass energy sources which currently account for more than 90 per cent of the total energy consumption. Firewood is the single most important energy source, accounting for 76 per cent of the total consumption, followed by agricultural residues (15 per cent) and dung (8 per cent). Some 43 per cent of Nepal's total area is covered by forests and of this total area of 6.3 million hectares about 4.6 million hectares are available for firewood production. It has been estimated that this area produces a sustainable supply of firewood in the order of 7.5 million tonnes, whereas usage is somewhere around 11 million tonnes. The remaining energy consumption is covered by fossil fuels (petroleum and coal) which have to be imported. Although these energy sources cover a mere 8.2 per cent of the total energy consumption, their imports have to be paid for by one third of the total foreign exchange earnings. Finally, hydroelectric power accounts for about one per cent of the total energy consumption.

Compared with most other countries, Nepal has few natural resources. Only one such source exists which is not only found in abundance but is also self-renewing:

the water flowing down from the mountains and hills on to the plains. It has been estimated that the theoretical potential of this energy source amounts to 83,000 MW, of which the economically exploitable hydropower is somewhere around 25–30,000 MW. At present only a very small amount (about one per cent) of this production potential has been developed.

An enhanced development of electricity production is essential in many respects, lack of power being a crucial element that restricts other development efforts. For this necessary energy development, thermal power and hydropower are the only realistic alternatives. The latter has many advantages: it can become the base for further industrialisation of the country; its introduction would diminish the use of diesel engines to generate electricity, thereby creating less pollution and decreasing fuel imports that are a drain on the national economy (indeed, it might even earn export income); and finally it might also lessen the pressure on forests, thereby preventing further forest depletion and erosion. In addition, the present massive dependence on firewood also places a heavy burden on women, who are responsible for its collection. It has been estimated that women nowadays have to spend as much as 20 per cent of their time collecting firewood. At present, women also have to spend a lot of time fetching and carrying water for household consumption, a burden which may be considerably lessened through an extended use of electricity.

According to the current Eighth Five-Year Plan (1992–97), the development of hydropower is a priority issue. Accordingly, the Plan states that "hydropower in particular will be developed as a new commercial energy base for the country's economical growth". The main objectives of the energy policy are described in terms of making the country more self-reliant and replacing imported energy while at the same time protecting the environment. It is also a major objective to integrate the private sector into hydropower development. The development of large hydropower projects is seen as a central element to an export-oriented strategy that will help the country make foreign exchange earnings. For the purpose of developing large hydropower plants, as much assistance as possible will be sought from multi-lateral and bilateral donors. Also medium and small hydropower projects will continue to be developed and here it is envisaged that the private sector will play a crucial role.

Besides hydropower there are also a number of alternative energy sources available, such as biogas, wind and solar energy. Biogas, which is a methane rich gas produced through anaerobic digestion of dung, has a big potential in Nepal. Theoretically, there is a potential to install more than one million biogas plants, while at present some 24,000 have been installed. Additionally, because of Nepal's latitude, solar energy has a big potential as has wind power energy generation. None of these alternative energy sources have so far been developed beyond the experimental stage. Especially in remote areas where hydropower development is difficult and expensive, solar and wind energy might be viable alternatives.

The development of alternative energy forms is discussed in the latest five-year plan and it is said that these will be encouraged. It is clear, however, that the development of large hydropower projects has received the highest priority and that the expansion of alter-native energy sources is dependent upon the will of the private sector to carry out research and make invest-ments; these in turn are affected by the political climate and electricity prices. Due to Nepal's mountainous terrain and the pattern of scattered and often remote settlements, it is in many cases simply not viable to supply energy through conventional means such as electricity via a national grid. Given this situation, the construction of micro hydroelectric power plants in the hills and the use of biogas in the Terai are promoted as viable alternatives. Thus, in many parts of the country, the focus has to be on locally based, small-scale means of providing energy to the population.

In recent years, expenditure from the energy budget has been heavily in favour of hydropower (for instance, from 1981 to 1994, hydropower projects received 99 per cent of the resources. Of this expenditure, 93.9 per cent went to large hydropower projects). During the Eighth Five-Year Plan, total expenditure on hydropower has been budgeted to Rs 30,384 million. This amounts to 20.9 per cent of the total budgeted resource allocation (up from 17.2 per cent during the Seventh Five-Year Plan). The alternative energy sources, including micro hydropower plants, have been allocated only Rs 1,650 million, of which Rs 1,050 million are allocated for biogas development. It is expected that public versus private expenditure will be in the order of 80:20 on the large-scale hydropower sector whereas opposite ratios will prevail in the development of small-scale or micro hydropower energy.

NORWAY AND NEPALESE HYDROPOWER DEVELOPMENT

The Norwegian Himal Asia Mission & United Mission to Nepal

The history of Norwegian involvement in the development of Nepalese hydropower began back in 1958 when Odd Hoftun, an electrical engineer, started working in Nepal for the United Mission to Nepal (UMN). The UMN is a Kathmandu-based association of Christian churches and missionary organisations from 20 countries; among them is the Norwegian Himal Asia Mission, which is involved in social work of various kinds in Nepal. Being an electrical engineer and having grown up in a country which, like Nepal, is endowed with large hydropower resources, Hoftun soon realised the impact that an exploitation of the water resources could have for the development of an indigenous Nepalese industry. From the very beginning, Hoftun was also convinced it was essential that the Nepalese themselves became engaged in the development of this resource, and, in insisting on this, he was indeed far ahead of his time.

Thus, in 1963, the Butwal Technical Institute (BTI) was set up in the small trading town of Butwal in northern Terai as an apprenticeship training centre. Here, four-year courses are provided for the training of general mechanics, welder mechanics and electricians. These courses are not only theoretical but also provide training in industrial environments. By 1995, 366 students had graduated from the institute and by this year, of the staff of 38 instructors, only one was an expatriate. Also in 1995, the courses had become so popular that the institute had 287 course applications, out of which only 35 were admitted.

The Tinau power plant
One of the reasons why Butwal was chosen as a training centre was that the Tinau river which flowed through the town provided an opportunity for a hydroelectric power project. This first, and rather small 1 MW project was in the hands of the Butwal Power Company (BPC) which was registered in 1965 as a company for the

production and sale of electric power. Construction began on the Tinau power plant in 1966 and was carried on in stages until finally, in 1978, the plant reached a capacity of 1 MW. After the Tinau plant was finished, the Himal Hydro company (HH) was formed in 1978 as a means to preserve and further develop the expertise gained, especially in the tunnelling field. HH has now developed into the leading Nepalese company undertaking construction work in hydropower projects. In 1990 the company had a total staff of 260 workers and 25 engineers of which 7 were expatriates.

The Andhi Khola power plant

Some four years later, in 1982, the BPC entered into an agreement with the Nepalese government to construct a combined power production and irrigation project, the Andhi Khola Hydel and Rural Electrification Project. Part of the water was used for irrigation while the rest went through a power house with a capacity of 5 MW. The project which involved more than two kilometres of tunnelling was successfully completed in 1991. As with the earlier Tinau project, a good deal of the equipment was obtained second hand from Norway and was then overhauled in Butwal by the Butwal Engineering Company (BEC), a mechanical workshop organised as part of the BTI activities. The project was supported by the Norwegian Agency for Development Cooperation (NORAD) with a grant of NOK 25.4 million. In 1991 the Andhi Khola power plant started production and has since produced an average of 35 GW per year.

The Jhimruk power plant

In 1987 Nepal sent an official request to the Norwegian government asking for assistance in financing a new 12 MW power plant in Jhimruk. The BPC as well as the

UMN reacted favourably to this proposal as it was seen as suitable for the continued training of Nepalese companies in the field. In May 1988, the Norwegian government informed Nepal that they were willing to support the project with a total amount of USD 19 million, a sum that was supposed to cover the entire production cost. The project was completed within budget in July 1994. The BPC was responsible for the construction and also operated the project during the one-year guarantee period. The BPC is now the permanent owner of the project.

The Khimti Khola power plant

The next (and so far the latest) project initiated by the UMN through the BPC is the Khimti Khola plant situated some 100 kilometres east of Kathmandu. This is a 60 MW project which is now under construction and when finished will increase existing Nepalese hydro-power capacity by about 25 per cent. The power from Khimti Khola will be badly needed as the planned giant Arun III power plant will not now be implemented due to the the World Bank's withdrawal of its promise to support the project with USD 700 million. The Khimti Khola plant will be owned by a company established specifically for this purpose, Himal Power, with the BPC and Statkraft SF as its main shareholders and Kvaerner and Asea Brown Boveri (ABB) as minority owners. A number of Norwegian companies in cooperation with Nepalese counterparts will be responsible for the construction work. Here, in a joint venture with Himal Hydro, Statkraft Anlegg is responsible for the construction work, while Kvaerner will deliver the mechanical equipment and ABB the electrical material; Nepal Hydro and Electric (NHE) will be their main subcontractor. It is expected that the total costs will amount to about USD

150 million, of which the Norwegian part, in the form of exports of goods and equipment, accounts for about one third.

The four main shareholders will provide slightly less than 30 per cent of the capital required for the project, with Statkraft contributing 73 per cent, ABB and Kvaerner 5 per cent each and BPC 17 per cent. The Asian Development Bank (ADB) and the World Bank have given 'soft' loans with an option to convert these into shares if in the future the plant becomes profitable. The remaining part of the costs will be financed through several loans divided equally between the ADB, World Bank and Eksportfinans. NORAD supports the project with some NOK 230 million and is guaranteeing the Norwegian export credits; it has also given soft loans and grants amounting to NOK 50–60 million.

The project has been delayed due to problems with the financing but it is now expected to be finalised by the year 2000. However, recently new problems have arisen since a road that was originally planned now has been cut out of the project. This has angered the local people who are now retaliating by blocking construction work which must be carried out during the coming dry season. If they cannot start as planned there will be further delays.

Private Norwegian Company Involvement

Statkraft SF

Statkraft SF which is owned by the Norwegian state has two independently operating subsidiary companies, Statkraft Anlegg (SA) and Statkraft Engineering (SE). In cooperation with BPC Hydroconsult, Statkraft Engineering has had the responsibility for engineering, project management and operation support for the Khimti Khola power project. Statkraft Anlegg is involved in the construction work of the Khimti Khola power plant. In this undertaking they cooperate with Himal Hydro (HH), the Nepalese construction company set up by the UMN after finalisation of the Tinau plant in 1978 (see above). HH is a well-functioning company experienced in the construction of several smaller power plants. For SA it has been essential to have access to this local partner since there are many practical tasks where a good knowledge of the local scene is essential. In exchange, SA increases HH's competence in project management and cost control, specifically within the fields of project leadership, risk management and overall efficiency. For example, while formerly HH had the capacity to finish 6–10 meters of tunnel per week, now this has now increased to some 40–50 meters through greater competence and the use of more modern equipment. SA is engaged in a training programme, instructing HH staff through so-called "on the job training". There have been some language problems but otherwise the training programme has been successful and mutually rewarding for both parties.

Among the Statkraft personnel interviewed, there is a general feeling that the Build-Own-Operate-Transfer (BOOT) model is a good one and should continue to be applied. However, there is a feeling of disenchantment with the way the the banks (the ADB and World Bank) operate. They were created to support the development of countries in the region but despite this they operate more like commercial companies. Through this BOOT model everybody can gain from hydropower development. They are also of the opinion that the development of water power is essential for the rural areas since this also gives scope for development of the road network. Together these projects provide an impetus for the development of local initiatives whereby people can stay in the rural areas, thus halting the flight to cities (especially Kathmandu).

Kvaerner and ABB

The Kvaerner and ABB engagement in the Khimti Khola power project, discussed above, is directed towards producing electrical equipment. The production will be divided between Norway and Nepal so that the Nepalese produce whatever they have the technical skills and capacity to do, with Norway producing the remainder. Part of the Kvaerner and ABB engagement is also to contribute to a training programme through which the Nepalese know-how in the field will be strengthened. This training programme is directed towards the NHE personnel and on the whole the cooperation has been smooth and rewarding for both parties. This has been so despite the differing ideological background of the two partners, the basic interest of the UMN staff being to support the Nepalese while ABB as a private company also has to earn money to be able to survive.

However, at times ABB found it frustrating to deal with the Nepalese government. For instance, the negotiations over the purchase agreement were time consuming; sometimes the right people did not turn up to meetings and nothing was achieved for a long time. It is thus considered necessary to simplify bureaucratic procedures and develop a more streamlined model for planning. Indeed, according to the ABB representative, the development of a legal framework to protect foreign investments is essential because the initial investment is expensive and time consuming. Political upheavals could, then, easily result in big losses unless there are defined laws and regulations that protect the investments. Finally, the ABB representative maintained that Norwegian environmental laws are a problem. Most probably, there would never have been any hydropower development in Norway if the laws had been as restrictive as they are now. Since all projects supported by NORAD follow these environmental regulations, this means that much money has to be spent on consultants trying to localise all possible effects on the environment.

Development of a Legal Framework

Norway has also been involved in an attempt to assist the Nepalese government in developing a legal framework covering the development and use of water resources. In 1993 NORAD received a request from Nepal to assist with this and for this purpose it was decided to make use of expertise from Norges Vassdrags-og Energiverk (NVE) in cooperation with the National Planning Commission (NPC) of Nepal. Previously, the use of water resources had been regulated by the Hydropower Development Policy and the Electricity Act both from 1992 but much had been dealt with by customary law only. A complete legal framework had never existed but, with the increasing development of water resources, the Nepalese authorities now felt the need to develop this framework in order to secure the use of these water resources in Nepalese hands and enhance the security for foreign investors. The work on developing the legal framework followed the decision to start building the Khimti power plant as this had the potential to provide a good situation for testing and correcting the new framework.

In their work, the NVE team initially cooperated with experts from the NPC and the Ministry of Water Resources (MWR); this partnership worked well and was satisfactory for all parties. However, following the shift in government in 1995, there was a reshuffle and for political reasons the NDC participants were with-drawn. Instead the NVE team was directed to cooperate with the newly-established Electric Development Centre (EDC), a lower-level organisation under the MWR which will have similar tasks with regard to electricity as the NVE has in Norway. A more active participation from EDC would have been desirable; the lack of this may have been due to the fact that they themselves did not gain directly from the project but there could also have been political factors involved.

Originally it was decided that the project should have continued through 1997 but the cooperation was to finish in November 1996 with a seminar to sum up the experiences. In the process, two laws have been written, a Water Use Act and an Electricity Law. The lesson to be drawn by these experiences is that institutional development cannot be done in a hurry and is dependent upon political factors which are often difficult to foresee. The choice of and continuity of relationships between cooperating partners are also extremely important since bonds of trust and confidence develop slowly and over time. When cooperating partners are exchanged due to political or other reasons, such bonds have to be de-veloped anew.

THE CIVIL ADMINISTRATION AND ITS FORMAL ROLE

In Nepal there are four governmental agencies respons-ible for the development of hydropower. The first of these is the Ministry of Water Resources (MWR) which is the main line ministry involved and has the sole responsibility for overall development of water resources, including electricity, irrigation, flood control and water-ways. Here, the MWR acts in coordination with the

National Planning Commission (NPC) and the Ministry of Finance.

Second is the Electricity Development Centre (EDC), which is the professional wing of the MWR and functions as one of its departments. It has been established to ensure the smooth execution of hydropower projects. This includes providing an environment that is conducive for the participation of the private sector. The Centre is chaired by the Minister of Water Resources and includes members from the various concerned ministries.

Third is the Water and Energy Commission (WEC), which is an advisory body to the Nepalese government in policy matters relating to the coordinated development of water and energy resources. The WEC also administers studies, surveys and investigations intended to provide a factual basis for policy recommendations and it renders opinions on issues related to the development of water resources. Within the WEC there is also the Water and Energy Commission Secretariat (WECS) which is responsible for recommending policy measures in the water and energy sectors. These are then forwarded first to the WEC for deliberation and then to the Nepalese government for adoption. Two organisations, the Canadian International Development Agency (CIDA) and the International Irrigation Management Institute (IIMI) assist WECS with professional services, training and research.

Fourth and last is the Nepal Electricity Authority (NEA), which is a public utility that has been designed to regulate the production, transmission and distribution of electricity in such a way that it becomes dependable and accessible to all. The NEA has three development objectives as follows: first, to identify and construct large and small hydropower plants to increase hydro generation capacity for domestic and export consumption; secondly, to extend and develop the transmission system into a national grid; and, thirdly, to extend the distribution network, particularly in rural areas, in accordance with the socio-political objectives of the Nepalese government. The NEA is the most important institution concerned with the development of hydropower projects but also has the responsibility for developing alternative energy sources.

It has been observed that although each of these four power development agencies have their own specific responsibilities, they have often tended to interfere with each other's duties, giving rise to much confusion. Hence, in the planning phase of power projects it has become commonplace to select a group of technicians and place them directly under the head of department in order for them to work directly with foreign consultants. This bypasses the ordinary bureaucratic procedures and aids the decision-making process.

THE NEA AND INDEPENDENT POWER PRODUCERS

It is the policy of the present government to open up the energy industry, including hydropower production, to private enterprises in such a way that free and equal competition is encouraged and moves are being made to address the inefficiency and corruption found in state-owned enterprises such as the NEA (at present this is is said to hold the world record in the number of employees per distributed kilowatt hour). It is also clear that neither the NEA nor the government has the funds to finance the large-scale hydropower development envisaged; additional funds will have to come from the private sector. The present strategy of the government is to find donors willing to support large hydropower projects like the Kali Gandaki project (now being implemented with support from the ADB). For small- and medium-scale projects, however, participation from the private sector is actively encouraged. Himal Power Ltd, which is to own the Khimti Khola power plant, is an example of this policy. Himal Power has signed a 20-year power purchase agreement with the NEA after which 50 per cent of the ownership of the plant will be transferred to the NEA. There has been apprehension that the power produced by the private sector will be too expensive. However, the power purchase agreement for Khimti Khola, which after protracted and difficult negotiations ended at USD 0.059 per kilowatt, clearly shows that private producers can deliver energy at competitive rates.

At present it seems that the NEA is reluctant to allow independent power producers an increased role, as it hopes that sufficient concessional funding from donors will become available to finance the future development of hydropower schemes. In the long run, the main function of the NEA will have to be to manage the national grid and distribution networks and to extend rural electrification. However, since there is an urgent need to develop hydropower and since the NEA already has the necessary schemes on the drawing board, ready to be developed, it seems realistic that for the next decade or so there will be a division of labour between the NEA and private producers.

The investment plan of the NEA covering the next two decades includes a number of large schemes (more than 100 MW in size) that it are to be built. There is also an alternative investment plan for smaller-size schemes, typically ranging between 25–80 MW, similar to the ones that are already operating in the country. A list of some of the schemes proposed is listed in Table 6 overleaf.

Table 6: Possible large and medium-sized projects

Large Schemes	Mw	Medium-sized Schemes	Mw
Kali Gandaki	140	Khimti Khola Phase 2	22
Arun III Phase 1	201	Bhote Kosi 1	64
Arun III Phase 2	201	Bhote Kosi 2	48
Upper Arun	335	Tama Kosi 2	68
Lower Arun	307	Tama Kosi 3	48
Upper Trishuli	210	Indrawati 2	33
Upper Karnali	240	Indrawati 3	25
Tila River	204		

In April 1996 the NEA called for suggestions from NGOs, government offices and persons on projects to be evaluated for possible implementation early next century. The list includes the projects listed in Table 7 opposite. By developing a number of these schemes through private hydro developers, the necessary public investment costs could be reduced substantially. Two of the schemes, Upper Marsyangdi and Modi Khola, are already under evaluation, the former by a Canadian partner and the latter by Statkraft and HH.

It has also been proposed that in each of the 75 districts in Nepal there should be developed small hydropower plants in the range of 7–10 MW. According to the calculations, economically such small plants could be highly competitive and would also offer independent development opportunities for the districts. The two UMN-sponsored power plants of Andhi Khola and Jhimruk could serve as models for such plants. Both are owned and operated by the BPC, they both generate

Table 7: Possible projects for further study

Region	Project Name	MW
Eastern	SB-0 Simbua Khola	37
	KB-A Kabeli A	16
	DD-1 Dudh Koshi	85
	DD-4 Dudh Koshi	82
	ST/ML-2 Mai Loop	60
	LK-4 Likhu	20
	TM-3 Tamur	53
	TM-3 Tamur	98
	TA-2 Tama Koshi	94
Central	RS-4 Rosi Khola	11
	LBH-1 Lower Bhote Koshi	132
	KH-2 Khimti	22
	UT-2 Upper Trishuli	210
Western	UMS-4 Upper Marsyangdi	73
	ST/AK-1 Andhi Khola	154
	RH-0 Rahughat	18
	MA-0 Modi Khola	14
Mid-Western	ST/S Sarada	75
	TR-2 Tila River	204
	BR-1 Bheri River	286
Far-Western	BG-4 Budhi Ganga	35
	SR-3 Seti	73
	KR-1A Upper Karnali	240

substantial revenues and together they now contribute 8 per cent of the total electricity production.

Many donors (both multilateral and bilateral) are involved in the Nepalese energy sector. The following table seeks to pinpoint the most important donors and their areas of interest.

Table 8: Donor involvement in hydropower development

Donor	Area of Interest
World Bank	Power Sector Efficiency Project
Asian Development Bank	Kali Gandaki Rural Electrification Project
CIDA, Canada	Institution Building in Water and Energy Sector
OECF, Japan	Kulekhani Disaster Prevention, Kali Gandaki Hydro Project
KfW, Germany	Arun III Hydropower Project (not to be financed)
FINNIDA, Finland	Expansion of Duhabi Multifuel
BITS, Sweden	Hetauda-Jusaha 132 KV TL
Danida, Denmark	Wind Power
Nordic Development Fund	Dumre-Besisahar 33 KV TL, Expansion of Duhabi Multifuel and 132 KV TL from Khimti to Kathmandu for the NEA
ODA, UK	Hetauda Thermal Refurbishment
JICA, Japan	Kathmandu Distribution Reinforcement, Kulekhani I and II Power House Rehab
Government of France	220 KV TL for Arun III (not to be financed)
GTZ, Germany	Small Hydro Master Plan
SNV, the Netherlands	Biogas
USAID	Micro Hydro Projects
UNDP	Wind Power, Micro Hydro Power

HYDROPOWER DEVELOPMENT AS A POLITICAL ISSUE

Finally, it should be mentioned that the issue of hydropower development (especially in the case of large projects) is a highly controversial one in Nepal today – an issue that can even lead to the downfall of governments and the consequent initiation of completely new policies.

The most heated public debate ever took place in 1993–94 and concerned plans to construct the Arun III power plant. Initially this giant project was planned to produce 402 MW but this was later reduced by 50 per cent. Towards the end of the 1980s the World Bank committed itself to the 700-million-dollar project provided that certain conditions were met by the Nepalese government. After much discussion, in March 1992, it was decided to cut the project to half its originally planned size and go ahead with the detailed planning. In order to comply with the financial conditions set by the World Bank for the construction of the power plant, Nepal was forced to enter into an Economical Structure Adjustment Programme (ESAP) under the guidance of the International Monetary Fund (IMF).

In 1993 an intense public debate began on Arun III and the conditions attached to its construction. Public hearings took place, alternatives were formulated and it was widely concluded that construction of Arun III was not in the interests of the Nepalese people. In September 1994, the NC government fell and was eventually replaced by a UML minority government. The new government refused to agree to those World Bank conditions relating to an increase in electricity tariffs and the construction of an access road. Without going into any of the details of the debate here it should just be mentioned that on 3 August 1995 the World Bank decided not to implement the project. Many different reasons were given for this decision but the opposition NC Party's view was that there was no doubt it was due to the policy of the Communist government.

In September 1996, the issue of a Nepal-India treaty on the sharing of water resources and integrated development of the Mahakali river was a hotly debated issue in Nepali politics. According to a treaty signed by the Prime Ministers of India and Nepal earlier in the year, the two countries will share equally the water resources of the river and Nepal is assured the right to export to India its electricity surplus produced by the planned power plant on the Mahakali river. At the point when the treaty was to be ratified in parliament, the Communist UML opposition, faced with growing internal opposition to the deal, threatened to reverse its original agreement and vote against the treaty because of some unclarified issues. Ultimately this threat was staved off and the government managed to achieve the necessary two-thirds majority, albeit with a narrow margin; the treaty was ratified on September 22.

What the latter case demonstrates with terrifying clarity, however, is not only the volatility of water and energy politics in Nepal but also the almost complete Nepalese dependence on India in energy matters. Any surplus produced in Nepal has to be exported to India, or at least via India; there is simply no way around it. This, of course, puts Nepal in a very vulnerable situation. If the energy production capacity is expanded to produce a surplus which has to be exported to or through India it is not certain that this can be done according to competitive world market prices but rather to prices dictated by India and its highly subsidised home market. Thus the Mahakali treaty is an important first step but has to be followed up by more general treaties in which Nepal secures unconditional rights to export to India any hydropower surplus produced at rates determined by the market value, not the subsidised one. Unless an agreement to this effect can be achieved, it will probably be politically impossible for Nepal to commit itself to large-scale hydropower development financed out of its national budget. Furthermore, if the UML is returned to power, it can be expected that Nepal's energy policy will shift towards favouring the production of smaller power plants designed to cover Nepal's own energy consumption needs rather than very large power plants producing for the export market.

SOCIAL AND ENVIRONMENTAL ISSUES

The environmental impact of power plants of course varies according to the size of the dam, the area flooded and the amount of water drawn from the river. In the Jhimruk project for instance it was planned that the entire flow would be diverted from the river during the times of the year when the flow into the causeway was less than what was required to operate the power plant. This situation typically occurs during the driest months of the year, in spring before the monsoon arrives. But also at this time the farmers cultivate a pre-monsoon paddy crop which requires a fair amount of water. Several of the villages also took their drinking water from the river. The project also affected the free migration (hence spawning) of a large number of fish species. Thus, an agreement on water sharing had to be worked out and a fish ladder built to secure free migration for the fish.

Another issue which can seriously affect local people is the question of compensation for land lost because of the project. Such compensation should be in the form of new land of equal quality, not just a sum of money. It is essential that a study about such environmental and social aspects is carried out early during the planning stage and not, as happened in Jhimruk, when construction is already well advanced. Furthermore it is essential that no project involvement by construction companies start before the Nepalese government solves the compensation claims. This is especially important because all too often the companies that develop the resources are blamed for deficiencies that are actually due to government inefficiency – to date, for instance, most construction contracts have not provided for environmental compensation.

As for the Khimti Khola project, the environmental and social impact will be minor since the part of the river that will be dry flows through a narrow valley with little cultivated land or habitation; only some ten households will be directly affected by the scheme. It will be necessary, however, to include a number of measures mitigating against those adverse effects that inevitably will occur. As in the case of the Jhimruk project, these include securing a minimum river flow during low-flow periods, installation of a fish ladder and measures (e.g. tree planting) to protect against erosion. Also in this case the Nepalese government will have to compensate affected farmers for their loss of land and buildings. The local people should also be given a share of the project's benefits in the form of power development in their area.

For both projects it seems that there has been an almost total lack of local participation in decision making. At best, the local people have been informed about the project and its effects rather than having had the chance to participate in and influence the decision-making process. On the other hand, it is not possible to achieve real local participation if the people are unaware of their rights and lack aspirations and knowledge. This becomes, then, a question of the long-term informal education of the local people.

Seen in a wider perspective there are many environmental advantages to be gained by hydropower development in Nepal. Firstly, there is a rapidly increasing demand for power which has to be met and rather than meeting this through the import of fossil fuels, Nepal should utilise its own natural resources. In the Terai for instance, the ADB has financed a large project to replace diesel pumps with electric pumps in irrigation schemes. Through irrigation the agriculture can be intensified and more food produced but the project makes little sense if there is no power to drive these electric pumps. In a regional perspective, there is much to gain if the seasonal river fluctuations could be evened out over the year by storing water in reservoirs; this would allow a more economical power generation and not only could monsoon flooding be reduced in the North Indian and Bangladeshi plains but also the flow could be increased during the dry period when irrigation water is often a very scarce resource.

CONCLUSIONS

It is possible to draw a number of conclusions and arrive at a few tentative recommendations out of this brief survey of Nepal's energy sector, the priorities of its government in this sector and the experiences of Norwegian involvement in Nepalese hydropower development; here the recommendations largely concern future inputs into the energy sector. Since hydropower is one of Nepal's few natural resources which are abundantly available and it is of central importance for the development of the country, this resource should be exploited. In the process, however, the expertise and the capacity of the Nepalese themselves to handle this development have to be in focus. To a large extent this strategy has already been employed. Steps have been made first to assist in the creation of a training centre and later the initiative has been taken to create a number of Nepalese companies which through training and practice can build up expertise in various aspects of hydropower development.

The UMN and its related companies first took on small projects whereby basic experience and know-how could be gained and slowly increased. More recently, the projects have grown in size and complexity in line with the capacity of the Nepalese companies to handle construction with a minimum of foreign assistance. However, while the earlier projects (Andhi Khola and Jhimruk) were of a size and complexity that could be handled largely by the Nepalese, the Khimti Khola is too large to be financed and implemented solely with donor money and using local competence. For Nepalese conditions, such power plants as the Khimti Khola (and even more the proposed Arun plant and other large-scale plants such as those in the NEA development plan) are large and complicated. Alternatively, the development of many smaller plants may open up other new and exciting possibilities. These can be adapted to local conditions and be vital to support and initiate further regional and local development.

In conclusion, it can be argued that on the whole the Norwegian engagement in the Nepalese energy sector has been fairly successful. As a result a model has been created whereby hydropower development can be accomplished while know-how is transferred to the Nepalese so that they can become less dependent on foreign assistance for future projects. The fact that such know-how can be transferred is due not only to the construction work itself but perhaps above all because of the UMN-sponsored companies through which the Nepalese know-how can be supported and enhanced. Through cooperation with these companies, private and foreign investments can now be channelled into the sector. In fact, without the growth of these companies, Nepal would have been completely dependent on foreign know-how. It should therefore always be a top priority for Norwegian inputs into the energy sector to support Nepalese competence building. This is the ultimate test against which all project proposals should be judged.

Given the great political uncertainty as well as economic and technical complexities connected with the development of large hydropower plants there.can be no doubt that the Norwegian contribution should preferably be weighted towards development of small- and maybe medium-sized plants. In the development of such plants, the technological know-how of Norwegian companies such as Statkraft, Kvaerner and ABB could play a decisive role. Another area where there is scope for input is in the field of micro-hydropower which when installed in remote, roadless areas may act as a catalyst for the local economy, especially if it is done in conjunction with rural development. Besides avoiding the politically highly controversial field of large-scale power plants, the development of micro power plants will therefore probably be of decisive value for other locally based development initiatives. Unfortunately there seems to be very little interest in small-scale rural electrification from either the MWR or NEA who prefer the more spectacular grand projects from which the country (and the staff involved) stand to gain foreign

Table 9: Estimate of regular and development-related government expenditure for the year 1996–97 (in Rs 000s)

Item	Regular	Devpt	Total
His Majesty and Royal Family	69,640	–	69,640
State Council	5,214	–	5,214
Parliament	109,496	–	109,496
Courts	230,558	–	230,558
Commission for Investigation of Abuse of Authority	5,550	–	5,550
Auditor General's Office	28,186	–	28,186
Public Service Commission	39,297	–	39,297
Electoral Commission	184,625	–	184,625
Attorney General	40,690	–	40,690
Council of Justice	1,455	–	1,455
HMG Secretariat	6,363	–	6,363
Council of Ministers	27,067	–	27,067
NPC Secretariat	48,374	34,791	83,165
Ministries			
Finance (MoF)	252,864	357,325	610,189
– Internal Loan Repayment	4,186,295	–	4,186,295
– Ext. Loan Repay't (Multilat'l)	2,795,424	–	2,795,424
– Ext. Loan Repay't (Bilateral)	859,941	–	859,941
– Investment (Internat'l Insts)	17,000	–	17,000
– Investment (Internal Insts)	–	8,491,503	8,491,503
– Other Investments	–	120,517	120,517
Supply	3,512	224,500	228,012
Housing and Physical Planning	90,001	1,691,407	1,781,408
Industry	232,021	268,941	500,962

Table 9 *continued*: Estimate of regular and development-related government expenditure for the year 1996–97 (in Rs 000s)

Item	Regular	Devpt	Total
Law and Justice	13,992	–	13,992
Agriculture	88,074	1,825,100	1,913,174
Home	2,640,415	4,393	2,644,808
Population and Environment	4,165	24,511	28,676
Water Resources	131,596	3,180,954	3,312,550
Works and Transport	171,756	4,667,101	4,838,857
Tourism and Civil Aviation	103,073	1,083,270	1,186,343
Foreign Affairs	527,431	–	527,431
Land Reform and Management	211,668	331,785	543,453
Women and Social Welfare	43,539	15,035	58,574
Youth, Sport and Culture	95,320	175,316	270,636
Defence	2,426,816	–	2,426,816
Forest and Soil Conservation	532,228	474,187	1,006,415
Commerce	17,570	34,000	51,570
Science and Technology	3,205	1,500	4,705
Education	5,079,010	2,680,287	7,759,297
General Administration	33,530	1,500	35,030
Information and Communic'n	541,018	49,559	590,577
Parliamentary Affairs	2,943	–	2,943
Local Development	27,339	4,074,983	4,102,322
Health	972,947	2,485,034	3,457,981
Labour	11,624	60,784	72,408

Source: Data drawn from Annex 4 of the *Budget Speech for the Fiscal Year 1996–97* (Kathmandu: Nepalese Ministry of Finance, 1996), pp. 46–47.

exchange money, prestige and profits. However, what is most needed in today's Nepal is to contribute to rural electrification and thereby provide a basis for encouraging local initiatives and subsequent development.

The Human Rights Sector

If the importance attached to human rights in Nepal is to be measured by the resources given to the government ministry most concerned with this issue, then one might only conclude that human rights in Nepal are accorded little importance. Out of the 47 government ministries in Nepal, the Ministry of Law and Justice receives the least money. Its share of the national budget for the 1996–97 fiscal year is only 0.02 per cent. In comparison, this share represents a mere 20 per cent of the Royal Yearly Support Grant (the *apanasje* or civil list).[1] Furthermore, out of the Rs 13,992 million which the ministry receives, all monies must be found from within the regular budget; nothing is available from development funds (provided by foreign grants etc). And perhaps symbolically, the minister himself (a renowned but elderly man who once fought for democracy in the early fifties, and ended up in prison with Koirala) is ethnically a Tamang.[2]

---

1   See Table 9 on pages 56–57 above.
2   The Tamangs are considered hierarchically very low even among the tribal alcohol-drinking castes. According to national caste laws (see below), they may not intermarry or even eat with Brahmins and Chettris. (Of course, in reality many do so, but then food may come from diferent kitchens.)

However, on a more positive note, the National Election Commission receives 10 times as much funds as the Ministry; furthermore, election monitoring is supported by DANIDA. It may be that this is prudent because problems relating to a free and fair election process are abundant in a country with open borders and no national identity cards.

Considering the low status and poor funding of the Ministry of Law and Justice, perhaps it is not surprising that Nepal's legal system is renowned for being highly corrupt and a hindrance rather than a help in the life of ordinary Nepalese citizens (i.e. the poorer strata of society). There is a common saying in Nepal that "more money changes hands in the lower or regional courts than in any other sector in Nepal". Indeed, the experiences of this writer (Harald O. Skar) after 8 years of working in Nepal serve to conclude that the rule for rural court cases is always, firstly, to be postponed and, secondly, to cost in terms of "help" rendered (nothing happens without money). Often land deeds (*Lal Purja*) are taken from the alleged offender as a kind of bail bond or guarantee while cases are pending. Cases involving poor people have been known to take decades to resolve, during which time land-use rights may have been lost.

There are basically three avenues for legal redress in Nepal:

- to relate cases to national law, although in various fields this is non-existent;
- to refer to local custom or practice, which of course varies among the 37 ethnic groups in the country (not to mention differences according to region and caste); or
- to refer to international laws that have been ratified by the Nepalese government.

NATIONAL LAW ISSUES

Hindu Legal Tradition

The most pervasive among Nepal's national laws is the Muluki Ain of 1854. This law was amended in 1963 but, according to general observers, "the amendments did not make the radical break with the past required".[1] In the Muluki Ain, relations of purity and caste, and of inter-group relations, are mapped out for everyone in Nepal. This regulates matters of conduct, inheritance, royal succession, property rights, relationships with foreigners, etc. A very good English translation of the Muluki Ain has been made by Andreas Höfer,[2] who also argues that the Nepalese legal system differs from that of India; in Nepal, the state assumes direct responsibility for regulating and maintaining the legal system, rather than merely acting as the enforcer of decisions made by Brahman priests. Thus Nepal, being the only formal Hindu country in the world, has a strong Hindu legal practice. This has a number of human rights implications. For instance, although the main Hindu legal tradition of *dharmashastras* (classical ethical and legal treaties) has now been secularised, there are still hindrances on women owning land within Nepal's national borders (see page 66 below).

International Law and National Practices

Nepal has so far ratified 14 international conventions, many of them after the victory of the pro-democratic

---

1   See Tulasi Ram Vaidya, *Crime and Punishment in Nepal, an Historical Perspective*, 1985.

2   Andreas Höfer, "The Caste Hierarchy and the State in Nepal. A Study of the Muluki Ain of 1854", in *Kumbu Himal*, vol. 13, no. 2 (pp. 25–240) Innsbruck: Universitetsverlag Wagner, 1979.

movement in 1990. The most recent ratifications include the:

- International Covenant on Economics, Social and Cultural Rights (ICESCR);
- International Covenant on Civil and Political Rights;
- Optional Protocol to the International Covenant on Civil and Political Rights (ICCPR);
- Convention against Torture and Other Cruel, Inhuman or Degrading Treatment or Punishment; and the
- Convention on the Rights of the Child.

Previously, Nepal had also ratified the:

- International Covenant on the Elimination of All Forms of Racial Discrimination;
- International Convention on the Suppression and Punishment of the Crime of Apartheid;
- Convention of the Elimination of All Forms of Discrimination Against Women;
- Convention on the Political Rights of Women;
- Slavery Convention of 1927, including amendments;
- Supplementary Convention on the Abolition of Slavery, the Slave Trade and Institutions and Practices Similar to Slavery;
- International Convention against Apartheid in Sports; and the
- Convention on the Prevention and Punishment of the Crime of Genocide.

Today there are many human rights organisations in Nepal using these ratified instruments on which to base their High Court cases against the government (see INHURED on page 73 below). A presentation of some of the cases pending will illustrate current human rights debates as well as the level of implementation of the instruments maintained above.

POLITICAL CASES

There are many ways in which international laws are used in Nepal to further political goals, especially as there is a lack of national laws to cover the intricate cases occurring in a "modern democratic country". For instance, it should be mentioned that on two occasions successive governments have dissolved Parliament (in the last instance, the Communist government's dissolution was hotly disputed and taken to court where the case was lost. This led to social unrest). Other court cases are those relating to the use of water resources. The first of these was the Tankpur Agreement with India where more than 50 individuals died during civil disturbances; the subsequent Arun III project also led to social unrest; and recently, in September 1996, the Mahakali treaty led to civil unrest that closed down Kathmandu for a day.

All of these cases were related to bilateral agreements with India and, in Nepal today, despite internal ethnic diversification, national feelings run high. The saying goes that if a government signs a treaty with India it will fall within a year. As the Mahakali treaty has only recently been signed (see the previous chapter on the energy sector), it will be interesting to see how the Communists may try to block these development projects with India. The end results of such cases often reflect the fact that political factors may change decisions even at High Court level. This is expected to happen if the Communists regain power. In that case, Supreme Court decisions may order Parliament to reopen the debate on already-agreed projects.

Nepal's ratification of international treaties relating to the environment has also been used in local court cases. Notably, several Supreme Court cases have cited the Nepalese accession to the 1992 Rio Convention as a basis for claims against the government. Cases are still pending especially in relation to mining.

Voting Rights

Today there are no identity cards in Nepal. Thus, with the open border to India, it is hard to establish who is a citizen and who is not – and who therefore may vote. Furthermore, in many rural areas, elections follow the "ethnic block voting" principle (i.e. ethnic groups tending to vote *en bloc* for one political party). It is no surprise, then, that ethnic groups who have been in conflict with each other over a longer period have shown a tendency to vote for different, opposing parties. This situation was typified by the electoral campaign during the 1995 general election among the Yadav ethnic group of lowland Nepal. The Yadav are also found across the border in the Indian state of Uttar Pradesh; here, indeed, there are Yadav ministers in the state legislature. However, even though they were from a neighbouring country, these ministers took part in campaigning in Nepal's election and, accordingly, were expelled. The ministers protested, stating that their constituents were "all Yadavs everywhere".

Control of voting in this 1995 election was based on census lists from 1984. Thus all those people listed had the wrong age stated (often the age being quite different to the person's true age). This resulted in some minors being able to vote (and accepting money to vote a specific way). On the other hand, many voters were prevented from casting their vote for a variety of reasons. In one district where this writer (Harald O.

Skar) was an official international observer, the census list was estimated to have only about half the names on it should have had. Moreover, because there was no proof of identity such as a voter's card or identity card,[1] when they turned up to vote, half of those who were on the lists were informed that they could not vote because "someone had already been there before them" (i.e. voted in their stead). Of the remaining 25 per cent of the voters, many had been bought. In some parts of Nepal bordering on India, neither rum nor women's *saris* were available in the market around election time. One party was said to have bought 10,000 *saris* in one night and the saying was that "one bottle of rum was equal to one vote".

The plight of bonded labourers with regard to voting should also be mentioned. This writer observed landlords going into the voting booths with their bonded labourers (one assumes this was to control how they voted). And in other areas bonded labourers were forced to remain working in the fields on voting day; no time off was given for voting (see section on page 67 below on bonded labour). Also, it has been estimated that most women in Nepal vote together with and in the same way as their men. The only good thing about elections, this writer was told, is that "this is handout time for everyone". All parties in all constituencies gave handouts, many poor being able to take advantage of this largesse.

Unsolved Legal Debates
Further, the State Offence and Punishment Act of 1989 and the provisions for death penalty in those laws can

---

1   Democracy is still frail in Nepal. Any project which might lead to voter identification would be a significant help in this respect.

be seen to conflict with the fundamental rights guaranteed by the constitution. This has not been resolved to date.

CIVIL RIGHTS CASES

Women and Property Rights

A case which is receiving much attention today is that of "equal property rights". Last year a Brahmin woman, Mira Kumali Dhungana, filed a case in the Supreme Court demanding that discriminatory laws still existing in the chapter relating to the division of family property in Nepal civil code should be repealed as they conflicted with international and national law as reflected in the new constitution of 1990. She won her case and the Supreme Court issued a mandatory order to Parliament to present a bill within one year. All parties, except the Communists (who are for equal rights), are divided on this issue (see the chapter based on interviews with political parties, starting at page 124 below). Many politicians fear their local constituency's opposition to this and some claim that women should not own land as this will change social traditions and patterns of marriage and ritual obligation. Anarchy is the word frequently used to describe the possible outcome. Some parliamentarians argue that parents should be able to share out their property according to their wishes and not according to legislation. This latter opinion is seen as a compromise. It is a step in the right direction as currently no women can own ancestral land in Nepal. With such a law women may own land with parental consent. As most land is ancestral in Nepal, this means that hardly any women have land registered in their own name today.

Bonded Labour and Slavery

It is widely known that bonded labour exists both in rural and urban areas. In urban areas it involves child labour in the carpet industry and the sale of female children to India for prostitution.

In rural areas, the slavery practice known as *kamayia* has been enforced for many generations. In this system, children inherit the debts of their fathers. (This is forbidden by law but exists in practice.) One of the problems is that although Nepalese law says that such practices are illegal, there are no provisions in the national law to actually punish the offenders. The question remains, how are such cases to be prosecuted? The absence of legal status keeps such cases from court.

The Nepalese government, including the Cabinet Secretariat, has demanded a court order to abolish the system of bonded labour still prevalent in the Kailali and Kanchanpur districts of far-western Nepal, specifically in the context of the Declaration of Human Rights 1948, the Convention against Slavery of 1927 (signed by Nepal in 1953) and the national Nepalese law of 1926. However, even though the Communist Government regarded this as an important issue, nothing has happened since the Congress and Royalist coalition took over. Cases are still pending in court and, until legal amendments have been procured, no violation is punishable. Many Members of Parliament from the far west have bonded labourers on their estates, and it is mainly due to the Danish project, BASE, and the Anglo-Norwegian Anti-Slavery Society that the issue has been brought to the attention of the UN, thus increasing the pressure on the Government. The number of slaves (bonded labour is a form of slavery according to the UN convention) in Nepal may be as many as one million.

The number of Nepalese children being sold for prostitution is now estimated to be around 50,000 to the Bombay area alone. Many return home with AIDS and even if they are not sick they are rarely reinstated in their families, as is often the case in Thailand. In Nepal, having been a prostitute, even unwillingly, means that you have become polluted as you may have had relations with low castes. Such shame is not as devastating for those in the *Bhadi*, a special caste group in Nepal which is linked to the trade of prostitution by hereditary occupational rights. Enforcement and cooperation with the Indian police have begun but progress is slow.

The Janajati movement (see page 71 below) has also been struggling to help the untouchables to secure civil rights. So far little progress has been achieved. Parliament has officially apologised for the delay, attributing this to monetary restraints.

Torture and Death

According to the *Human Rights Year Book 1996*,[1] in 1995 there were eight cases of killing by state employees in Nepal. Five people were shot dead by forest guards for encroaching on state forest land and the rest by the police. There were 100 reported cases of torture, 95 of these of people held under state detention, 3 in private hands and 2 when in the hands of political parties. It is commonplace that suspects are beaten after arrest to extort confessions. The types of torture reported include beating, piercing nail joints with pins, hanging upside down, squeezing with iron bars, beating on the soles of the feet with pipe, etc. Twenty-five people have died while in police custody or prison, 21 of these being adult males, one an adult female and one a female minor. The *Year Book* cites the causes of death as torture,

---

1   See page 73 below for fuller details on this *Year Book*.

inadequate medical care whilst sick, suicide and various natural causes.

Figure 2: The rising incidence and frequency of human rights violations in Nepal, 1992–95

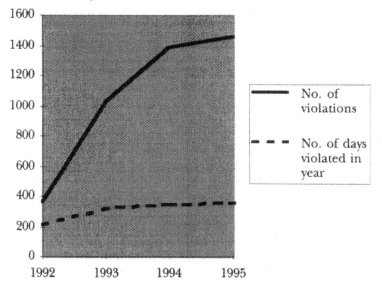

Source: Data adapted from *Human Rights Yearbook 1995* (INSEC, Kathmandu), Appendix 12, p. 1.

Civil Servant Rights

In 1991, almost 2,000 civil servants were dismissed from their jobs and only about 200 were later reinstated. It was not until 1995 that a case in the Supreme Court led to a judgement that the arbitrary dismissal of civil servants was against the fundamental right of equality within the nation. Today civil servants are often moved and dismissed due to political affiliation and caste. This is part of the system of *Chakary* and political leaders strongly support the tradition of *Apnu Manche* (that is, personnel recruitment through favours). Nepalese bureaucratic offices are often full of people waiting their turn. However, many are not there to ask for help or favours but to pay homage and display obedience. They may wait in the office of an official for weeks on end, hoping for the chance to do him a favour, which later must be repaid. Current court cases concerning civil servants demonstrate a new tendency away from such practices.

Habeas Corpus

It took a 1996 Supreme Court order to outlaw the practice of "holding persons in detention without clear and un-ambiguous orders from competent authorities". The Supreme Court's intervention was required due to the frequency of politicians and influential people without legal grounds ordering detention of their enemies and other people.

Another issue dealt with in the Supreme Court con-cerned random and over-severe punishments. A case decided that "no convict will be awarded more sentence than prescribed by prevailing law". This case reflects the fact that poor people rarely win in rural courts, unless they are in someone's favour.

Indigenous Peoples and Ethnic Issues in Nepal

One of the current general conflicts in Nepal is rooted in the difference between Buddhists and Hindus within the kingdom. Nepal, being a Hindu country for many generations, has recently had a national count on religious affiliation. Although official figures have not been published, it has leaked that the non-Hindu group now probably constitutes more than 50 per cent of the population.

The bulk of those who are not Hindu are Buddhists. The Buddha was actually born in Lumbini in Nepal (see Skar 1985 for a further debate). The Buddhist groups are mainly dwellers of the middle hill ranges (that is, tribal peoples such as Rai, Limbu, Gurung, Sherpa, Tamang and also refugees from Tibet). After 1990 they formed a Janajati movement, a movement of all nations, also called the *adivasi* or indigenous movement.[1] For a while there was widespread fear that they would form a political party, which would have been illegal (as, according to the 1990 Constitution, no party can be formed according to religious or ethnic affiliation). However, the three main parties all adopted generally pro-Janajati policies thus pre-empting the creation of such a party at election time. Recently, however, the Congress Party, after forming a coalition with the Royalists, has become very pro-Hindu and the Communists have accordingly become very pro-Janajati.

To defuse this situation all parties agreed to tolerate the Janajati movement in its peaceful endeavours towards furthering ethnic understanding amongst all ethnic groups. They formulated a special programme for the improvement of the situation of downtrodden communities and indigenous peoples. Parliament approved the establishment of a college and, additionally, an ethnic cultural centre/ethnographic museum was planned and supported by NORAD. All ideas furthering the understanding of the cultural complexities in Nepal have had multi-party support.

The Media and Freedom of Expression

Newspapers are mainly printed in Nepalese, Hindi and English. The 1990 Constitution of Nepal guarantees the rights of access to information and a free press. This is in huge contrast to the *Panchayat* times before the advent of the democracy movement. New newspapers are said to be established almost daily and the press is

---

1   *Jana* = "many", *jati* = "caste" or "tribe", and *adivasi* = "down-trodden".

basically uncensored. The government media (state newspapers, state radio and the state-monopolised television channel), however, have been frequently accused of only presenting the views of the government parties. Accusations of censorship of some programmes have also been heard (for instance of popular news programmes and the nine o'clock programme for human rights which was first established by the communists). The private press is equally biased and a measure of objectivity can only be obtained by reading a variety of newspapers.

There is probably a large amount of truth in accusations of censorship of major political events. The number of political deaths during last year's elections was hushed up (probably 10 died in party clashes). In addition, the Supreme Court recently supported the request of Advocate Bal Krishna Neupane for information that had been suppressed concerning the action plan signed between Nepal and India in 1993 which regulated the development of water resources.

LOCAL HUMAN RIGHTS, NGOs AND POLITICS IN NEPAL

There are presently about 30 human rights NGOs in Nepal, some examples of whom are detailed below.

FOFHUR

The Forum for Protection and Promotion of Human Rights (FOFHUR) is the oldest human rights organisation in Nepal. At election time it functions as a coordinator of the other election-monitoring organisations. It is a well-run organisation led by a charismatic and well connected General Secretary, Krishna Prasad Siwakoti. It is an organisation of concerned professionals rather than a grass-roots affair.

INSEC

The Information Sector Service Centre (INSEC) is one of the leading grass-roots organisations working for human rights in Nepal. It has carried out pioneering studies into the problems of slavery in Nepal and its reports have been submitted to the UN working group on this issue. Today it is one of the few groups working on the question of the untouchables. During the period of Communist government, INSEC had its own human rights radio programme.

NORAD has supported INSEC with the publication of the *Human Rights Year Book*, which appears in both Nepalese and English. This book was also used as a model when establishing a similar year book in Burma. However, neither Congress nor the Royalist Party (RPP) wanted to be included in the book's section on comments from the political parties. Furthermore, some of the articles favour a UML viewpoint. Despite this, it is so far the only real publication on human rights in Nepal and, as such, it is widely used by the national and international community.

INHURED

The International Institute for Human Rights, Environment and Development (INHURED) is an organisation of professionals who specialise in the use of international organisations applied to Nepalese conditions. They have given priority to to the analysis of World Bank projects. INHURED has also led the campaign against large hydro-power developments in Nepal during the recent Arun III and Mahakali debates. It is the only Nepalese NGO recognised by the UN (ECOSOC) as an observer. INHURED's director, Gopal Chintau, has suggested that a Norwegian-funded project be implemented concerning the environment and the utilisation of water resources.

INHURED also functions as the secretariat for Child Rights Watch Nepal, a national coalition of NGOs working for children's rights. The organisations represented are the Child Development Society, the Child Welfare Society and INHURED, with UNICEF Nepal and Redd Barna (Norway) as observer members. The activities of Child Rights Watch Nepal benefit from support to Redd Barna.

INHURED also has a dynamic Women's Rights Department which recently formed a "Beyond Beijing Committee". They were planning a large-scale conference on "Beyond Beijing" for February 1997.

DECENTRALISATION AND DEMOCRACY DEVELOPMENT EFFORTS

For decades the human rights sector has benefited from a number of bilateral and multilateral donors. Lately, however, projects have focused on decentralisation and democracy. The Danes have been involved in writing the constitution of Nepal after the revolution of 1990, and both the Danes and the Americans have contributed by supporting democracy at a decentralised level. The first foreign individual to be part of the Nepalese government's planning commission is Danish. He sits on the Commission on Decentralisation. Below will be mentioned the DALAN project sponsored by DANIDA and the LOGOS project sponsored by USAID. Both relate to decentralisation and democracy-building at VDC level. They have proved highly successful and may provide links that can be used by other donors, such as the Norwegians. Finally, UNDP's programme in this sector will also be touched on.

DALAN (Danish Assistance for the Strengthening of Local Authorities in Nepal) is intended to support the

LDTA (Local Development Training Academy). Basically, it has been helping to improve the performance of local authorities in terms of increased resource mobilisation and utilisation of available resources. At the end of the four year project, it is "expected that all members of VDCs and DDCs in Nepal will have a basic understanding of the rights and duties and law of local government". By educating people in their rights, it is hoped to achieve a more just society over time.

LOGOS (Local Government Strengthening Project) is designed to assist DDCs, VDC user groups and citizens in the process of democratic decision making at the local level. Each project VDC has a resident LOGOS staff member and a District Coordinator at district level. LOGOS technical assistance consists primarily of "professional workshops and other training activities". LOGOS also has a complementary grant programme.

UNDP's NEP/92/027 project, also known as the Democracy Strengthening Project, has been implemented through the National Planning Commission in 20 districts since the revolution in 1990. The project's main contribution has been to revive the District Profiles which were originally conceived under the Decentralisation Act.

In 1996 DANIDA recognised that both projects had "run into difficulties" but also recognised that new donors in the field may learn as much from their own mistakes as from the successes of their predecessors. Thus for an agency starting out in this sector, it is important to look into the possibilities of cooperation.

CONCLUSIONS

Although public democratic institutions and the civil rights situation do not seem to have improved substantially over the last few years, political rights are much developed and this may pave the way for further changes. There can be a tendency towards political abuse in the NGO sector. However, NGOs as a whole are useful in spreading aid to many organisations, although a monopolisation of interests should be avoided. A possible combination of DANIDA and USAID in electoral issues would, however, be interesting as a continuation of the Norwegian Bar Association's efforts.

Another method of furthering democracy would be to support the peaceful understanding of ethnic diversity, as in the case of the Ethnographic Museum endeavour (see page 71). Any such efforts, however, would need to be co-ordinated between a multitude of donors.

The Education Sector

Historical Background

Before the first Nepalese revolution of 1950–51, education was accessible only to the Royal Family and the ruling classes (Brahmins and Rana families). After this time, the dissemination of modern education concepts was slow. It was not until 1971 that the educational system was formally centralised and a uniform curriculum was developed.

In 1990, the year of the second revolution, Nepal endorsed the Jomptien Declaration (from the Bangkok World Conference on Education) and a Nepalese delegation attended the World Summit on Children held in New York. Having agreed that from now on the goal should be "education for all", the first comprehensive National Education Plan was drawn up that year. The plan aimed to raise the primary school attendance rate from 64 per cent (31 per cent for girls) to 100 per cent, and to increase the completion rate from 27 per cent to 70 per cent within the next 10 years.

National Policies

National policies in the educational sector are set by the National Education Commission (NEC), which was established in 1990. There are two main objectives:

- providing access to education (more schools), and
- improving the quality of education (better trained teachers, greater curriculum development and more textbooks).

The Eighth Five-Year Plan (1992–97) set the following general goal: to provide access to education for 90 per cent of 6–10-year-old children by the end of 1997. For that purpose 2,025 new schools were to be established which necessitated the training of 35,000 primary school teachers, including 8,000 new recruits.

STRUCTURE OF THE EDUCATION SECTOR

The Nepalese education sector has three basic levels: primary, secondary and higher. The national education structure is illustrated in Table 10 opposite.

Primary Education

In the primary education sector, the government has committed itself to make this level of education (grades 1–5) accessible to all children aged 6–10 by the year 2000. In fact there is currently running a compulsory primary education experiment in two Nepalese districts (Kavre and Chitwan) amongst childen of school age. Currently primary education is provided free of charge.

An issue hotly debated in Parliament at the moment is whether primary education should be provided in the mother tongue. As there are 37 ethnic groups in Nepal with approximately 50 local languages, this point has become important to the Janajati Movement (see page 71 above).

In April 1994, according to the Ministry of Finance's *Economic Survey 1996–97*, the number of students enrolled in grades 1–10 in the kingdom's schools was recorded

Table 10: National educational structure

Grade	Level	Normal Age
1		6
2		7
3	Primary Education	8
4		9
5		10
6		11
7	Lower Secondary Education	12
8		13
9	Secondary Education	14
10		15
11	Higher Secondary Education	16
12		17
13		18
14	Higher Education (University)	19
15	General Professional,	20
16	Technical, Sanskrit	21
17+		22+

Source: Adapted from *Ministry of Education, Nepal* (Ministry of Education, Keshar Mahal, Kathmandu, 2nd. ed., 1996), p. 3.

at 4,136,000. The tendency is for children to drop out after two to three years in the rural areas.

Secondary Education

The secondary education sector is divided into three parts: lower secondary (grades 6–8), secondary (grades 9–10) and higher secondary education (grades 11–12).

After having completed 10 years in the educational system, students may sit a School Leaving Certificate (SLC) exam, the passing of which automatically qualifies the student to work as a primary school teacher. This practice has been institutionalised since 1934. As there is a shortage of teachers in Nepal today, the passing of the SLC exam guarantees a job. In addition, a higher secondary education level, the so-called "10+2", has been introduced and a new curriculum and texts have been developed with help from the World Bank. So far, there are approximately 75 "10+2" facilities (private and public), including the university campuses.

Today, as many as 67 per cent of all university students study for only two years. Accordingly, it has been decided to separate this group of "10+2" students from the "advanced educational group". Monetary resources and teachers for the newly-created higher secondary level educational facilities are to be taken from the universities and supplementary funding is being sought. The results will hopefully be better teachers for primary schools, more advanced secondary schools and an easing of overcrowding at Tribhuvan University. A new Institute of Education has been established and this will help the Ministry of Education with its reforms.

The approximate numbers/ratios of students in the primary and secondary schools can be seen from Figure 3 opposite.

Higher Education

The university structure in Nepal is highly centralised around Tribhuvan University, which has its main campus at Kirtipur, Kathmandu. Since its establishment in 1959, the number of educational facilities under the university has rapidly increased. Today there are 150,000 students studying at 61 campuses, as well as at 132 affiliated

Figure 3: Number of students enrolled, 1986–96

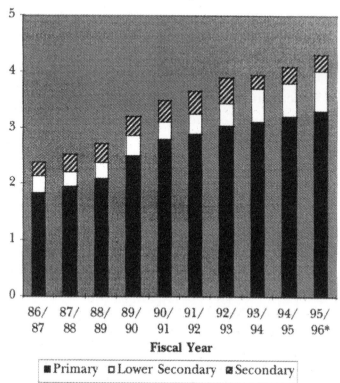

Fiscal Year

■ Primary □ Lower Secondary ▨ Secondary

*Note: estimate only.

Source: Based on *Economic Survey Fiscal Year 1995–96* (Ministry of Finance, Kathmandu, 1996), p. 127.

campuses and Tribhuvan University-recognised high schools. There are as many as 5,400 professional staff employed within this structure.

Tribhuvan University offers degrees up to PhD level although the educational content varies between departments. The number of students who partake in the higher secondary education outside of the university structure is rapidly increasing, so much so that after 2005 the university will no longer provide for higher secondary education ("10+2"). Tribhuvan University has

9 faculties in all, each with a wide number of institutes and fields:

- Humanities and Social Sciences
- Management
- Law
- Education
- Science and Technology
- Engineering
- Forestry
- Agriculture and Animal Science, and
- Medicine (including university hospitals).

In addition the university has 5 research centres:

- Centre for Economic Development and Administration (CEDA)
- Centre for Nepal and Asian Studies (CNAS)
- Research Centre for Applied Science and Technology (RECAST)
- Research Centre for Educational Innovation and Development (CERID), and
- Curriculum Development Centre.

As for the private sector, Kathmandu University was established in 1991 as a non-profit university. Today it caters for work-based education such as business administration, accountancy, engineering, etc. The Mahendra Sanskrit University (at Dang) is the only public university which is also independent. It receives a basic grant from the government and functions as a Royal Hindu foundation, maintaining Hindu values and standards in the country. Parliamentarians have debated whether a Buddhist university should also be established. So far an inter-ethnic centre is seen as a solution. (The Buddhist issue is also discussed in the chapter on Human Rights – see the discussion from page 70 onwards.) Some other universities are also currently under construction, namely Purvanchal University in East Nepal (at Biratnagar), a western university in Pokhara, and another in Chitwan in lowland Tarrai.

THE SECTORS IN FINANCIAL PERSPECTIVE

The Ministry of Education receives the largest share of Nepalese government expenditure. It is estimated that in 1996–97 the Ministry will receive approximately Rs 7,759,297,000, which is twice as much as received by the Ministry of Health. Of this amount, a third is set aside for project development. The tables in the Appendix (derived from the statistical section of the Ministry of Finance's 1996–97 budget speech) show that, from the total Nepalese national budget for 1996–97, (estimated at Rs 7,565,615,000), education expenditure is slightly down to 13.7 per cent (see Figure 4).

The Ministry has begun to view education as a part of an ongoing process rather than an end result. It is the foundation upon which skilled and semi-skilled manpower can build to set up business or at least become self-reliant.

Teachers' Education

Teachers are viewed today as rebuilders of the educational system. Emphasis is being placed on improving the quality of education by raising the educational level of teachers. Previously, to qualify as a a teacher, a person did not even need to have a SLC pass.[1] However,

---

1   Regarding the School Leaving Certificate, see page 79 above.

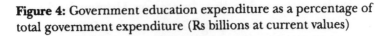

Figure 4: Government education expenditure as a percentage of total government expenditure (Rs billions at current values)

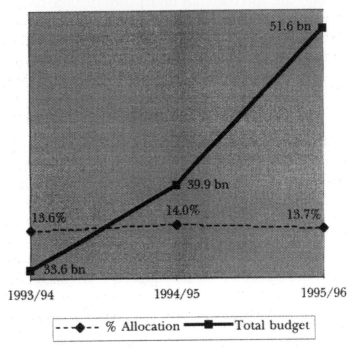

1993/94   1994/95   1995/96

- - - ◆ - - % Allocation ——■——Total budget

Source: Adapted from *Ministry of Education, Nepal* (Ministry of Education, Keshar Mahal, Kathmandu, 2nd. ed., 1996), p. 31.

it is now intended to make a minimum of "10+2" education compulsory in order to become a teacher. This means that the 40,000 teachers (approximately half of the total) who were hired without formal qualifications now represent a serious problem.

The Private Education Sector

One of the largest problems in the Nepalese educational system today is the gap in academic results between private and public education. Every year more than 100,000 tenth-grade students sit for the SLC examination. Some 80 per cent of the students who pass are from private schools, mainly male students from the Kathmandu valley. The same situation arises in the higher education sector. Here private universities are admitting an increasingly high percentage of first class students. Kathmandu University today also offers business courses and engineering studies geared directly to highly-paid jobs. Thus, despite high fees, it is not unusual for whole villages to pool their resources and select one of their young to go there. It is of course of immeasurable value for a village to subsequently have access to, say, a qualified lawyer belonging and beholden to that community. A large segment of the middle class receive their education in neighbouring countries. Previously, rich Nepalese students would go to the USA to study medicine, but lately the differences in the standards between the two educational systems have made this impossible.

THE WORKINGS OF THE MINISTRY OF EDUCATION

The formal structure of the Ministry of Education is illustrated in Figure 5 overleaf. However, one may basically say that even though it appears to have all the appropriate divisions and departments, efficiency at all levels is low. A DANIDA report summarised the views of all those we interviewed:

> Today MOE can in many ways best be described as a personnel department controlling, administrating and regulating teacher conditions and can only to a lesser degree be seen as a technical education expertise ministry. 90 per cent of the Ministry's budget is used for teachers' salaries, not on curriculum and new structure planning. (1996: 70)

In reality the "educational scenario" in today's Nepal consists of an "alternative structure" built up around current

Figure 5: Organisation of the Ministry of Education

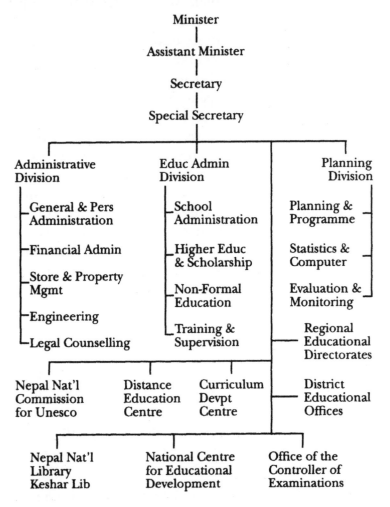

Source: Adapted from *Ministry of Education, Nepal* (Ministry of Education, Keshar Mahal, Kathmandu, 2nd. ed., 1996), p. 2.

major "projects". This structure is totally donor based and high quality personnel will generally be found here. All the projects were initiated around 1992–93 and some, such as the BPEP (see page 88 below), are now into their second phase. This "alternative structure" replicates the levels of the MOE. The "alternative structure" is illustrated below.

Table 11: Education programmes and their donors

Programme	Donor
Universities	Private Nepalese funds
Participatory Management Development Programme	UNDP
Higher Secondary Education Project (10+2)	Funding presently sought
Secondary Education Development Project (SEDEP)	ADB
Primary Education Development Project (PEDP)	ADB
Basic Primary Education Project (BPEP)	ODA (loan), DANIDA, UNICEF, UNDP and JICA

Source: H.O. Skar

This structure is where we find "the educators" of Nepal, and it exists as a supplement to the MOE structure. A different donor has taken responsibility for each level and DANIDA's involvement in the BPEP is regarded as a model by other bilateral donors. As we have seen, this is also where donors have flocked. The BPEP and "10+2" are currently requesting Norwegian participation, as is the PEDP. These will be described in more detail below.

DONOR ASSISTANCE IN THE EDUCATION SECTOR

Project Forerunners

Although international agencies such as UNICEF have sponsored educational projects in Nepal since 1971,

systematic large-scale donor assistance in the educational
sector did not begin until 1981 with the ERD SET
project in East Nepal which covered five districts in the
Seti zone. The project was supported by UNDP, Unesco
and UNICEF up till 1992. Another project, the Primary
Education Project (PEP), was initiated by the World Bank
and ran for 10 years, developing curriculum, textbooks,
teacher training and some construction of schools. These
were the forerunners of the projects mentioned below.

BPEP

The Basic Primary Education Project (BPEP) was initiated
in 1991 as part of the Master Plan for Primary Education
for 1991–2001. The estimated cost of the project was
USD 118.5 million. The BPEP is referred to as a project,
but in terms of coverage and the nature of its activities, it
has more the nature of a national programme. The BPEP
is a donor co-ordinated project within which different
donors support various components of the project. For
example, the World Bank supports school construction,
recurrent costs and resource centre construction while
DANIDA supports resource centre development (a research centre is planned for every Village Development
Committee), women's education, and non-formal rehab-
ilitation/maintenance. For its part, UNICEF supports
curriculum and textbook development plus non-formal
education and Japan's JICA supports supplies of school
con-struction materials.

  The BPEP has had an enormous impact in a short
space of time. It has provided additional classroom space
for about 300,000 students and non-formal education
for more than 170,000 adults and children. With such
achievements it is not surprising that the government is
eager to finance a second stage of this project. Stage
one was activated in 40 districts in Nepal, while the next
phase will focus on the remaining 35 districts.

The Eighth Five-Year Plan aims to provide one female teacher for every primary school in Nepal (currently 22,000). The BPEP alone has already provided 2,750 such teachers. However, the BPEP progress report for 1995 mentions that despite this great achievement "70 per cent of schools still lack a female teacher". This could be explained by the fact that the general social structure of Nepalese society does not encourage marriageable women working away from paternal homes in independent jobs.

Financing

The main portion of funds from the donors goes to the Treasury which in turn passes funds to projects. This means that project finance must firstly be approved by the Planning Commission, which then instructs the Ministry of Finance to supply the Ministry of Education with the appropriate amount. The money is then channelled to the Directorate for Education and on to the Regional Directorates where project activities actually take place. UNICEF is currently experimenting with direct financing of project activities as accounting is slow and can take up to three years (see page 120 below). Such a decentralised approach was previously adopted in Nepal in 1994 by the Communist government with the block grant approach. Much of the money in East Nepal was used to rebuild schools.

Higher Secondary School Project ("10+2")

This project is in the pipeline. Currently, it is the subject of hot debate in Nepal as university teachers will be required to take leave of absence to participate in the programme. It is expected that university teachers will need to take leave for five years before going back to their positions. The Director of "10+2", Dr. T.R. Khamia, explained to the author (H.O. Skar) that the project could only be a success if he could offer these teachers a higher salary than at the university.

As the "10+2" initiative will deprive the universities of more than 60 per cent of their students, budget re-allocations must also take place. In Nepal today, there is the paradoxical situation where university studies are free (as is primary education), but secondary education is not. The Eighth Five-Year Plan aims to provide free secondary education and, according to Minister G. Raj Joshi, this will also be reflected in the Ninth Five-Year Plan.

Administrative Comment

During the author's interview with the Minister, Mr. Joshi primarily stressed the need for help in this sector. He maintained that, "while all the donors want to participate in the BPEP success, our main challenge is to strengthen teacher training through a reformation of our secondary educational system". The Director of the BPEP, however, maintains that such training is also provided within the BPEP and PEDP projects (for fuller details on the PEDP project, see below) and informed me confidentially that he will submit his suggestions for financing to the Minister. The Director of the BPEP, Mr. Laxmi Nath Shresta of the PEDP, and Dr. T. R. Khamia of "10+2" are personal friends which facilitates coordination between the projects.

Primary Education Development Project (PEDP)

The PEDP was introduced "to provide school teachers with training opportunities and exposure to improve content and pedagogical aspects ... to train all untrained primary school teachers and raise their competence and skills" (MOE: 1996:22). However, a recent DANIDA review (1996: 76) concluded that "the effort concern-ing teacher training has been the least successful". The director of the project was recently replaced and the new director, Mr. Laxmi Nath Shresta, stresses the need for support of the Primary Teacher Training Centres which have been built up under the project. This should be seen in the context of the new "10+2" strategy. Teachers previously only needed ten years' education and an SLC pass (sometimes even less) to get a job but in the future they will require the "10+2", that is 12 years of education. A serious challenge remains in upgrading the educational level of those with only an SLC pass and those who were hired at an earlier date without even that qualification.

The Current Situation of Primary School Teachers in Nepal.

In the primary education sector, there are about 22,000 schools, 3.2 million students and 85,000 teachers (out of whom only 34,000 are trained). Of those who are trained, only a few have specialised education in addition to the SLC pass. One study (CHIRAG 1995) shows that at the present rate of teacher training it will take more than 60 years to catch up. Presently, each class has an average of 95 students per teacher. Salaries are low and the high turnover rate causes serious problems when trained staff leave development projects. As the loss of staff is virtually continuous, some projects have established an ongoing educational effort within their project structure.

CONCLUSIONS

Even if Norway does not wish to become a large-scale implementor in the educational sector in Nepal, it would still be prudent to invest in the BPEP structure. This is the view of Mr. Nepal, who is in charge of the Planning Commision. Furthermore, if other large-scale donors invest in the "10+2" strategy, this is likely to have a big impact on the quality of teaching in the future. However, before any investment can be made in the "10+2" alternative, the Nepalese government must specify its monetary policy regarding this new endeavour. In addition, a system for direct financing of the new "10+2" private and public institutions must be considered.

The largest challenge facing Nepal in the near future is not the provision of education *per se* but rather the provision of occupational training that in turn can help to alleviate unemployment. Thus, all those interviewed, including the Minister and UNICEF personnel, stressed the need to strengthen vocational training. Although non-formal education is part of the BPEP framework, this mainly consists of adult literacy programmes financed by DANIDA. A secondary vocational training effort within high schools is currently being developed as an alternative to "10+2". This may become an interesting and important development arena. From an analysis of teacher-student ratios we can see that, although the national government has provided approximately twice as many primary schools as the private sector, there are roughly the same number of secondary schools in each sector. Furthermore, the statistics illustrate that, in those rural areas farther away from Kathmandu, there are twice as many private secondary schools as there are government schools. This is indicative of the problems facing the government in providing education for all.

The Health Sector

BACKGROUND

A recent report by Sigrun Møgedal (DIS: March 1996) reviewed the development of the health sector in Nepal. This is a highly recommended report, the main points of which are detailed below.

Development in the health sector is currently on the decline. Today the health infrastructure only treats about 20 per cent of the population with facility-based primary care. Equity and access to basic care are crucial issues for the health sector. There are severe gaps in the infrastructure and major underfunding. More efficient utilisation of available funds and additional funding are required. The types of external support are just as important as volume. Rapid privatisation with an urban focus is threatening to undermine public efforts, particularly in attracting scarce personnel. Measures are needed to limit curative specialised care to an equitable cost. There is a need for government to play a more proactive role in order to set an example to the private sector. Priorities and mechanisms for mutual accountability between public, private and NGO sectors must be established. There is a considerable develop-ment potential in the Norwegian NGO efforts in Nepal, as well as in the multi- or bilateral arrangements currently being developed with UNICEF, UNFPA and WHO.

Sigrun Møgedal's concluding recommendations are (1) to primarily use the multi-bilateral channel of project support in the current year and (2) to support infrastructural developments at the first-level referral units (primary health centres and district hospitals) through the Ministry of Health (MOH). Other long-term alternatives include:

- Capacity building in public institutions to manage the public/private mix. (partners WHO/WB).
- Strengthening health manpower management within the public sector (with WHO).
- Providing recurrent budget support for the MOH.
- Providing recurrent budget support for UMN hospital operations during its transition to the MOH.
- The regional hospital option (NUFU project) to provide postgraduate training of specialists. (This alternative does not conflict with the general recommendation to focus on the government's plan for primary health).

In this study we generally agree with Møgedal's recommendations ([1] and [2]), but seriously doubt whether Norwegian aid should be used for any of the efforts outlined under long-term alternatives. Basically we believe that the strengthening of management capacities under the MOH has been tried unsuccessfully by many others before and it is doubtful if a Norwegian effort could produce better results. Furthermore, we consider that it would be unwise to provide recurrent cost allocations to the MOH at the present time when the Ministry has such a low absorption capacity for funding (see below). Rather we argue that a review is needed regarding the possibility of health personnel training to be used in the newly-built decentralised structure (a possible partner of Redd Barna). Such a review should include an analysis of the UMN health efforts to see if this channel may provide further possibilities.

CURRENT SITUATION

Below we present a short review of the current situation, taking into account interviews with central authorities, doctors, international NGOs and NGOs. We also make some observations towards an understanding of the problems involved for donors in this sector. Here we focus on the capacity of the Ministry of Health to plan and execute decisions. Today all donors specify that the MOH is the most bureaucratic and inefficient ministry of all the 47 ministries in Nepal.

Finance

From anticipated government expenditure for the fiscal year 1996–97, we can see that the MOH receives approximately Rs 3.5 billion or 6 per cent of the annual budget and about half of the educational sector's share. More than two thirds of MOH expenditure is on development while recurring costs only represent one third. Many donors are presently being asked to partake in recurrent cost sharing, even though other ministries, such as the Ministry of Education, appear to manage much more efficiently than the MOH.

A recent (1994) study on "Budget Restructuring to Achieve Human Development Goals in Nepal" by the National Planning Commission concludes that the reason for the lack of support to the health sector in general is "partly because the government investment programme lacks well defined priorities, and the social sector, particularly health and water supply, maintains a low profile".

A simple assessment of the budgetary allocation to the social sector in the first two years (1992–93) of the Eighth Five-Year Plan period indicates that not only will allocations fail to meet physical targets but also they are likely to fall short of the financial targets themselves. Expenditure on health in these first two years was just 26 per cent of the targeted five-year outlay. Actual expenditure is estimated to have reached only 20 per cent. If this trend is followed, estimated expenditure will be at approximately 76 per cent this year.

In short this means that the MOH is in receipt of only 6 per cent of government spending, and even then it is unable to absorb and make use of more than two thirds of these reduced funds. (Spending on health in Norway is also about 6 per cent but this is with a developed hospital sector and a functioning health care system that has been built up with substantial funding over many decades.)

Furthermore, the budget restructuring review also concludes that disbursement of foreign aid has been less than 50 per cent of the aid commitment in recent years. This is a trend exhibited in the social sector generally. In the health sector, disbursement has varied between 18.8 per cent to 71.83 per cent over the period 1980–92. This in itself is an indication that the planning process leaves much to be desired (see Figure 6 opposite).

The Ministry of Finance's economic survey of 1995–96 for the health sector shows that, out of the total foreign aid disbursement of Rs 105.4 million in 1990–91, only 3.3 million consisted of loans while the rest was in grants. In 1994–95 the ratio was similarly low with Rs 416.2 million being spent and only 30 million being loans. In contrast to other sectors (such as education, which today is the recipient of about two-thirds of total spending in loans), the health sector basically relies on grants

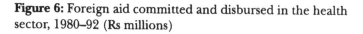

Figure 6: Foreign aid committed and disbursed in the health sector, 1980–92 (Rs millions)

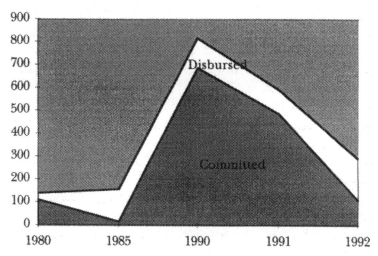

Source: Adapted from *Economic Survey Fiscal Year 1995–96* (Ministry of Finance, Kathmandu, 1996), Table 4.11

or donor gifts like the JICA's equipment grant to the Teaching Hospital or the USAID contraceptive grant of over USD 2 million a year. The Nepalese are obviously reluctant to divert their own resources to health.

Managerial Capacity and Planning

Møgedal in her report stresses the need to increase the planning capacity in the MOH. There is no doubt that this should be a priority. Until recently the Germans with the World Bank had a capacity training scheme operating. Then USAID and UNFPA diverted resources towards the same goal. Lately the ADB took over and finally today UNICEF has developed a Multiple Indicator Surveillance Strategy which they are currently asking the Planning Commission or MOH to assume responsibility for. So far the Ministry has resisted but progress is being made regarding the Planning Commission. Even if, however, better planning is achieved, there still remains the problem of enforcement by employees and bureaucrats. Planning capacity is one element which is needed (to ensure budgets are not overspent by 800 per cent, as demonstrated in Figure 6).

However, the managerial skills that can implement plans are probably even more important. We seriously doubt whether such skills may be acquired at present given the managerial culture found in Nepal today. This is a general problem in Nepal but it is particularly virulent in the health sector. For example, doctors who are assigned to a medical post rarely take up their posts if they are outside the Kathmandu valley. A recent bill currently being debated in Parliament recommends that all doctors serve at least one year in the rural districts. However, law enforcement is generally very selective in Nepal, depending on caste, party affiliation and regional contacts. A similar problem exists regarding basic health personnel in general since payment for health field services is very low. The MOH rate for TA/DA (travel and daily allowances) is only Rs 100 per day (NOK 10,-). The shortage of personnel, particularly in regional areas leads to a lack of real information on which plans for future actions in the health sector can be based. Much planning is therefore based on guesswork whilst trying to ignore the the acute problems in the rural health care.

The Ministry, Primary Health Centres and the VDC Sub-Health Posts

Figure 7 opposite illustrates the organisation of the health sector. As in the case of the Ministry of Education, on the surface it seems to be well organised with referral units at all levels, ranging from the sub-health post level to the zonal hospitals of which there are nine in five zones. Much of the criticism of the system, however, centres around the fact that few doctors are available

Figure 7: Organisation of the health sector

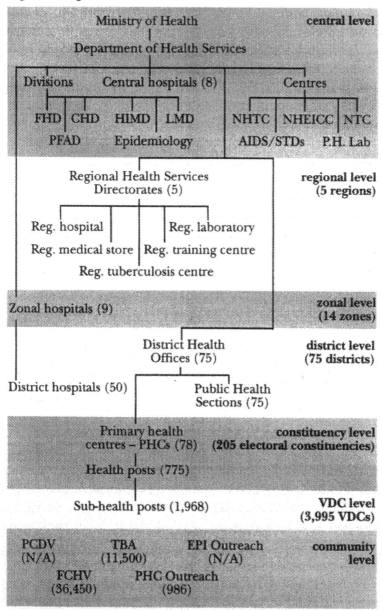

Source: Adapted from *Annual Report, Department of Health Services, 1994/1995* (Ministry of Health, Kathmandu, 1995), p. 12.

for referrals, even at district health level, while lower-level staff have little or no western medical training. At the level of the primary health centres, health personnel trained in the *ayurvedic* (Hindu) tradition are prevalent and do a relatively good job under the circumstances. However, in general, one has to travel to a district or zonal capital to actually see a doctor. Doctors should be found at electoral constituency level in the Primary Health Centres (PHCs) (refer Figure 7 above). However, only 78 out of 205 constituencies have PHCs today and staff shortages make it almost impossible to make use of existing physical facilities.

Besides creating PHCs at electoral levels (for obvious reasons), a new focus on decentralisation (see below) is leading to a level of health care being constructed at the lowest level of public administration in Nepal, namely the so-called VDC (Village Development Committee, previously known as *panchayat*). This new level of health service is known as the sub-health post (SHP). The 1996 annual report for the Department of Health Services (DoHS) states: "according to the Institutional Framework of the DoHS/MOH, the sub-health post (SHP) functions as the first contact point for basic health services". However, the sub-health post is only the first contact point from an institutional perspective. In reality it is a referral centre for the volunteer cadres of TBAs (11,500), FCHVs (36,450 Female Community Health Volunteers) as well as community-based activities such as the PHC (Public Health Care) and EPI (Expanded Programme on Immunisation), Outreach, and home visiting. Today there are approximately 2,000 sub-health posts and the plan is to expand this service to all 4000 VDCs. (Each VDC has nine wards in Nepal, and each ward normally consists of one village or, if the village is large, a part of such.)

◆ ◆ ◆

Following these introductory remarks, we now present a review of the health sector and its achievements during the last year.

PLANS AND TARGETS

The targets of the Eighth Five-Year Plan are as follows. The government's number one target is to create 20 new Primary Health Centres and 600 sub-health posts between 1996–97. The appropriate sites have now been selected. The tendency to give priority to basic health care is also said to be reflected in the Ninth Five-Year Plan. The World Bank has given Nepal a soft loan of USD 26 million over the next four years (under its programme for population and health) towards infrastructure developments, namely sub-health posts and

Figure 8: Infant mortality rate, 1950/60–1995/96 (per thousand)

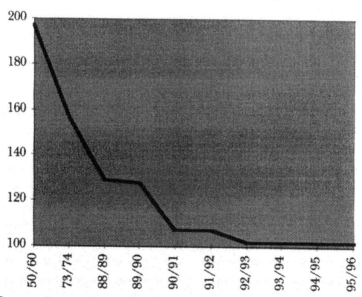

Source: *Economic Survey Fiscal Year 1995–96* (Ministry of Finance, Kathmandu, 1996), p. 135

Figure 9: Child mortality rate, 1973/74–1995/96 (per thousand)

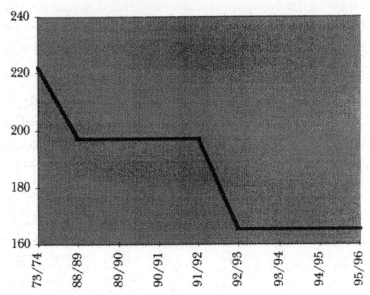

Source: *Economic Survey Fiscal Year 1995–96* (Ministry of Finance, Kathmandu, 1996), p. 135

health centres at constituency level. The hospital structure has not been considered.

The goal of all national health plans has so far remained the same every year, namely the "attainment of the highest possible level of health by all Nepalese people". Let us now thus refer to the targets the government has set for the year 2000.

Infant mortality dropped sharply from the 1950s but its rate has been largely static in recent years (see Figure 8 on previous page). The target is for the rate to be reduced to 50 per 1,000 from the present 102 per 1,000.

Child mortality dropped steadily from the 1970s but here too the rate has been largely static in recent years (see Figure 9 above). The target is for the rate for children under 5 years to be reduced to 70 per 1,000 from the present estimate of 165 per 1,000.

Figure 10: Crude birth rate, 1950/60–1995/96 (per thousand)

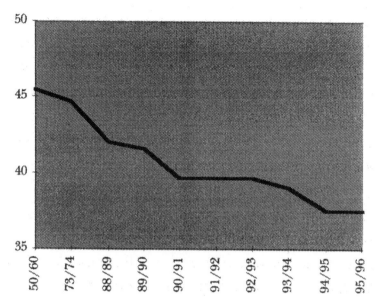

Source: *Economic Survey Fiscal Year 1995–96* (Ministry of Finance, Kathmandu, 1996), p. 135

Total fertility has been steadily dropping since the 1950s but its rate has been largely static in recent years (for crude births, see Figure 10 above). The target is for the total fertility rate to be reduced to 4.0 from the present estimate of 5.8.

Maternal mortality remains high. The target is for the rate to be reduced to 4.0 per 1,000 from the present estimated rate of 8.5 per 1,000.

Life expectancy has improved dramatically since the 1950s, in part due to the improved crude mortality rate (see Figures 11 and Figure 12 overleaf). The target is for life expectancy to be raised on average to 65 years from the present estimated average of 53 years.

Strategies proposed to achieve these goals by the year 2000 are described in detail in the *Annual Report* by the Department of Health Services. However, the following survey of the year 1995–96 may serve as a more accurate indication of development since it records actual achievements as well as goals and dreams.

CURRENT STATUS OF ACHIEVEMENTS AS AT 1995–96

Vaccination

In line with the call from WHO to eradicate polio from the globe by the year 2000, a vaccination programme for children was to be conducted by observing a special immunisation day throughout Nepal. The Norwegian Minister of Health would assist at the event since Norway has donated funds towards this campaign. Such endeavours appear to be relatively effective in Nepal as

Figure 11: Crude mortality rate, 1950/60–1995/96 (per thousand)

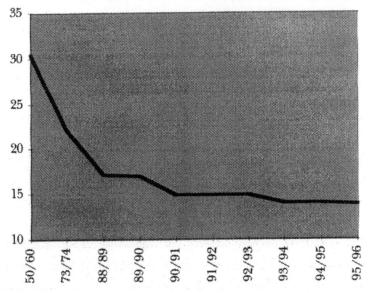

Source: *Economic Survey Fiscal Year 1995–96* (Ministry of Finance, Kathmandu, 1996), p. 135

far as school children are concerned, although school attendance rate is still low, especially for girls (see chapter on education). The problem of bonded labour in the rural areas (estimated to affect approximately one million people) also prevents children from taking part in such social services. However, investments in vertical programmes like this, where donors pool and channel resources via international NGOs, are likely to yield good results with few implementation difficulties.

Malaria, Kalajar and Japanese Encephalitis

These mosquito-borne diseases are today endemic in the lowlands of Nepal. Malaria was almost eradicated for a short time after a WHO program in the 1960s, however, today it is once again on the increase. The government target of spraying insecticide twice a year in "vulnerable

Figure 12: Life expectancy, 1950/60–1995/96 (years)

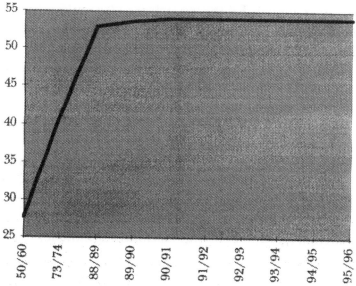

Source: *Economic Survey Fiscal Year 1995–96* (Ministry of Finance, Kathmandu, 1996), p. 135

areas" has been implemented but other areas also require spraying. Against the target of collecting blood samples from approximately 365,000 people, only 36.5 per cent of this figure was achieved during the first 8 months of the year.

Family Planning

Family planning services were provided to 202,885 individuals during 1994–95 and during 1995–96 the number was down to 135,571. Condom dispensers provided by USAID have been placed in all VDCs with sub-health posts, and both UNFPA and the World Bank are providing services to the new level of health facilities. Prenatal and post-partum services treat around 130,000 women each year.

Hospitals and Health Centres

So far there are 775 health posts and 78 Primary Health Centres at electoral constituency level (see Figure 7 above). Comprising the next level of hospitals are 50 district hospitals and 75 district health offices/health sections. Lastly, there are 9 government zonal hospitals at the now abolished zonal bureaucratic level (zonal commissioners and police are now only regional with hospitals being the only zonal institutions left). However, private hospitals are being created in Pokhara and in the Kathmandu valley as well as the government cancer hospital in Baratpur, in the Tarai lowland and Primary Health Centres (PHCs). The number of *ayurvedic* hospitals has now reached 172, including 5 hospitals during the past 8 months (see also page 108 below).

With regard to PHCs (at electoral constituency level), 20 new units have been established. 600 sites have been located for VDC sub-health posts, although there is insufficient funding for infrastructure investments, especially as donors are concerned about personnel and training.

Those that are in operation do not seem to give out any feedback and therefore the Multiple Indicator Surveillance lack data at this level.

The number of hospitals and health centres increased by 20 per cent during the first eight months of 1996, the number at time of writing being 3,722 (for the long-term trends, see Figure 14 on page 114). There are about 1,500 doctors, of whom approximately 1,000 work in the government sector. Skilled manpower in the health sector is estimated to have increased to 28,120, which is up by more than 3,000 since 1995. Every year approximately 100 new students are admitted to medical studies.

A closer look at the Pathan Hospital run by the United Mission to Nepal is worthwhile. Its channel of aid and its general approach serve as good examples. This model, which is built around eye care hospitals, together with an independent national trust (the Nethra Jothi Sang), has been a success mainly due to the strong-minded individuals involved. Whether this model can be replicated, however, is debatable. With the current emphasis on primary health care, such specialised hospitals are a low priority for the government. This may cause problems for all those in need of such services and lead to more privatisation and a continuation of the "medical patient exodus" to India.

Ayurvedic and Traditional Medicine

Besides the many hospitals now in use (172 so far and rapidly growing), a Development Committee has been formed to strengthen the Singha Durbar Vaidaykhana, a hospital teaching facility of *ayurvedic* medicine (i.e. that following the Hindu tradition). It is important here to remember that at the last population census, 51 per cent of the population was considered non-Hindu.

Any emphasis on this sector by the current government is viewed by some as "sanscritisation" or India-friendly. Sub-health post and health post personnel may in the future be increasingly recruited with such an educational background.

A summary of major achievements, reflected by health indicators since 1950–60, is presented Figures 8–12 above.

Other Achievements

Lastly, a number of other significant achievements are worth mentioning. Two mobile health clinics came into operation last year. A scheme to make the nation self-sufficient in drugs and medicines has also been success-ful but Indian production is still cheaper in many respects. Iodised salt has been transported under the goitre pro-gramme, but has only provided about one quarter of the 2 million quintals required. Problems with re-iodisation of Indian salt have arisen since salt loses its iodine content after storage in hot climates. And finally the Nepalese government has started subsidising part of the medical expenses of senior citizens over 75 and children below 5 years of age.

POLICY ISSUES

Local Community and Decentralisation

To achieve the goals listed from page 102, the most important strategy is to focus on the community. The CPM/UML Communist Party began the "Build Your Village Yourselves" (BOVO programme) and provided all the Village Development Committees with a block grant of Rs 300,000 to start their own development programmes. The Communists' BOVO Programme won a tremendous amount of good will in the rural areas.

Today every party in power is fighting to outdo the Communists by providing more money and services in the districts. (Part of this process involves bringing democracy to the county level. This is supported by DANIDA with about DKK 20 million in aid, and UNDP is currently restructuring all its programmes to follow this trend.)

In order to extend health services to the communities, the previous focus on health posts (of which there are now 775) was not seen as enough. Therefore levels both above and below the health post were created. Above the health posts, the main focus was on expanding the available health care at each electoral constituency and finding doctors to go there. Below the health post, the priority was the creation of so-called sub-health posts (with volunteers) at each VDC. In other words, the local level political emphasis focusing on constituencies and the decentralisation efforts started by the Communists became fully operational.

Remarks

As in the educational sector, the VDC level is favoured in a decentralised approach to development in the health sector. Here, there is differentiation between political and medical reasons for decentralisation. The Communists started decentralisation for political reasons in order to attract the votes of the poor people and the present government has followed suit due to the Communists' success. Besides political reasons for favouring aid disbursement at the VDC level, there are other arguments based on health indicators. Studies show that the main causes of child death in Nepal are pneumonia and vitamin A deficiency. A community health project in Jumla has been able to reduce the child mortality rate by 50 per cent at VDC level through education on basic hygiene etc. Along with measures to provide better access to clean drinking water, it is hoped that the community approach will give the best value for money. However, in the project mentioned above, the government was not involved and local participation was very high. In contrast, the government system has been described as an over-centralised and fragmentary system without transparency or accountability in relation to the users. The quality of services, inadequate deployment and supervision of all categories of staff and the lack of functioning referral systems have led to a general under-utilisation of the "primary health care services". Furthermore, the question remains what will happen to those that actually need hospitalisation if the primary sector is neglected to the degree that it is in present-day Nepal.

PRIVATISATION

Another serious challenge for the health sector of Nepal is the current process of privatisation. In the National Health Policy Strategy Plan (Part 4.6 of which refers to the private sector), the government appears to favour facilitatation of privatisation rather than regulation. It is stated that "the private sector will be encouraged to provide specialised and general curative health services within the Kingdom". Regulation of the private sector would also be contrary to the Nepalese government's general policy of structural adjustment. Nepal initiated the Enhanced Structural Adjustment Programme (ESAP) in 1992–93 with the objective of:

> Attaining a higher sustainable real growth through comprehensive structural reforms and better utilisation of foreign aid in high-return projects. The programme has promoted commercial orientation for public enterprises by completely eliminating subsidies and privatising all public enterprises, with the exception of 11 related to public utilities.

The health sector is no exception to this policy.

When interviewed by the author, a group of wealthy businessmen in Kathmandu expressed a willingness to invest in the health sector; indeed many had already done so. They presented the following picture of the situation: health facilities were poorly developed in the neighbouring provinces of India, Uttar Pradesh and Bihar but at the same time many Nepalese citizens currently travelled to South India or Delhi for health check-ups. Thus, as they saw it, there was an expanding market for health services to be developed. Many had already invested in new private clinics in the Kathmandu area and

Figure 13: Total health expenditure by sector (per capita)

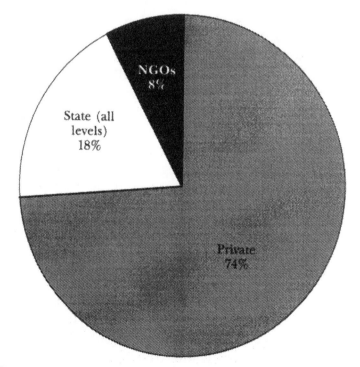

Source: Based on Nepalese government data

hotels were being converted into private nursing homes. Such ventures were very lucrative investments, with over a hundred homes already being established. However, whilst few agreed on the government's decentralisation strategy, they were not worried about possible government interference in what they saw as their business. (Politicians need to tread carefully in dealings with the Nepalese business community as it is so small, elitist and well-connected. As such, it tends to dictate rather than accept legislation.) As over 80 per cent of the population is still rural, a large drift to the capital is expected where there is also an abundance of health personnel. This is viewed as a field for expanded investment.

In discussions on privatisation with the Minister of Health, Arjun Narasingha K.C., he agreed with the long term evaluations of development which were carried out by the business community, but was very reluctant to see donor money go into the private sector. He considered that "private sector care will develop rapidly enough without the foreign donors. What we need is district and rural health services, and the education of personnel to make the government achieve its obligations to the Nepalese people". He further emphasised that "if NORAD wanted to go into regional health or hospital development, such endeavours would be looked upon favourably, if the end result was more qualified health personnel". The Planning Commission, however, seemed rather more politically attuned to the new topic of decentralisation. Again it is a question of the quality of services rendered, as Figure 14 opposite shows.

This figure shows that skilled manpower (excluding doctors) is down by almost 1,000 since 1994, while the number of service centres (namely rural sub-health posts) are increasing at a steady rate (this is due to the World Bank loan of USD 26 million towards this.) The question

Figure 14: Extension of health services, 1985–96

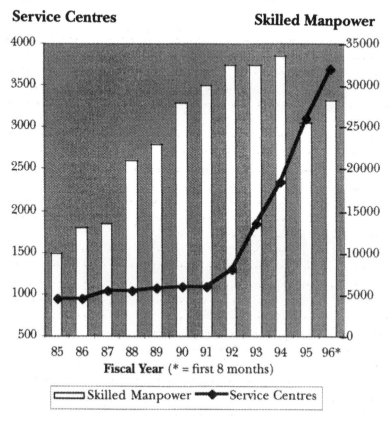

Service Centres   **Skilled Manpower**

Fiscal Year (* = first 8 months)

Skilled Manpower   Service Centres

Source: *Economic Survey Fiscal Year 1995–96* (Ministry of Finance, Kathmandu, 1996), p. 133

remains who will provide services in all the new facilities that have been built? According to DANIDA, for example, a health post in Dunai in Jumla has now been vacant for three and a half years following the completion of construction.

Both the education of personnel and the means to motivate them to remain in rural posts are thus the main challenges in the years to come. The relationship between efforts in primary health compared to curative

services etc. is mapped out in the pie chart below. This
is the situation under the present government and the
focus on VDC sub-health posts would no doubt be greater
if the Communists were to take over.

Figure 15: Health sector budget under the Eighth Five-Year Plan
(1992/93–1996/97)

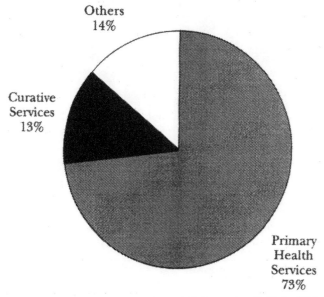

Others
14%

Curative
Services
13%

Primary
Health
Services
73%

Source: Based on data from *Health Information Bulletin*, Vol. 9, 1995

CONCLUSIONS

The Health sector in Nepal is badly organised, over-
bureaucratic and difficult to work with. Its absorption
capacity of foreign aid is very low. The comments on working with government ministries that follow in the next
chapter are for the purpose of advising the Norwegian
government that donors in this sector should probably
favour short-term project-orientated aid rather than a
long-term programme approach. Specific activities that

can be closely monitored at each step should thus be the first priority. The development of a similar donor structure to that used in the Ministry of Education may be the solution in the short run, although here we run into the problem of sustainability. Many donors such as USAID avoid the problem by direct financing through consultancy firms (see page 119 below). A separate structure has also been built by the United Mission to Nepal with the Pathan hospital in Kathmandu and other efforts in many regional areas. This may prove useful, as may the established network relations of Redd Barna in this sector.

The possibility of co-financing with bilateral donors such as USAID and German Aid should also be pursued if investing in the primary or regional health sector. It is also important to develop relationships with international NGOs such as UNICEF and WHO.

General Observations on Donor Experiences

The observations below relate to aid in general but have been placed after the Health Sector chapter as most of the examples are from this sector.

EXPERIENCES WITH THE NEPALESE GOVERNMENT

Donor funds are channelled through a variety of Nepalese ministries. Therefore funds from the same country and in the same sector may be channelled through different ministries according to interpersonal relations and experiences. For example, German bilateral aid is basically processed through the Ministry of Development, while funds of the German UNICEF Committee are channelled through the Ministry of Welfare. Donor relations with the latter Ministry seem to be more positive.

The large number of ministries in existence in Nepal today (47) makes it difficult for donors to decide which ministry to approach. Moreover, functions move; for instance, sections formerly part of the Ministry of Education have today been passed to four other ministries: those of Social Welfare, Women, Culture and Sports. In addition, further sections of the old MOE are being transferred to the Ministry of Local Development. The

Ministry of Women, headed by Lila Koirala, who is related to the last Congress Party Prime Minister, does not appear to be very powerful. Employees of the Ministry of Local Development who are working on credit schemes for rural women have refused to join the Ministry of Women. Everyone agrees that the Ministry of Education is also very weak. This is why DANIDA, UNICEF, the World Bank and UNDP have chosen to set up an alternative structure through the BPEP project (see page 88 above). However, this is not really a long-term solution, as one basically ends up doing all the work without any co-operation.

Furthermore, the Ministry of Health is generally viewed by everyone as "a disaster" (to quote various sources) – "Lots of talk, lots of agreement but no action". For instance, the sum of USD 1.5 million set aside for a country-wide drug programme has been untouched for 2 years and thus the bilateral donor is considering withdrawing the funds. Furthermore, support of sub-health posts through UNICEF has encountered severe setbacks. Due to problems arising from the frequent movement of staff, the Ministry of Health recently agreed to a moratorium on staff transfers from project areas for a year but proceeded to do so anyway three weeks later.

This problem seems to be present in all ministries and reflects the role that party politics play even at very low levels. Personnel are basically being transferred from rural to central areas for reasons of political promotion. A UNICEF worker claimed that the only way to really work with the MOH is to do everything for them, but what will then happen with sustainability? Another possible way forward was to use the now decentralised VDC (Village Development Committee) system to fund projects directly at this level.

Politics and Bureaucracy

In Nepal the saying goes that "everywhere, everyone is politicised". At election time, teachers, health officers, programme managers and ministers are changed. Each party has a network of "loyal workers" who are recruited individually through the "*aphnu manche*", or "*chakary*" approach, namely taking care only of those who are loyal to you in return). It is socially acceptable for such workers to be promoted as often as possible by those in power for so long as their power lasts. In each ministry, the party politics associated with there being a coalition government may thus also dictate sector policy. Further criteria for promotion are by membership of an ethnic group, caste or region. If you belong to the "correct" religion, caste, ethnic group and party, then qualifications or performance are not relevant in obtaining a job or promotion. If a donor agency or educational institution has vacancies, ministers will soon telephone to recommend their candidates. If such candidates are not promoted then delays in bureaucratic procedure may be expected. Favouritism and patronage are seen as a part of everyday life in Nepalese politics.

USAID views concur with those of UNICEF and in order to make projects work in the health sector, they now use private Nepalese contracting firms to execute their projects. (USAID uses a firm called MAS, Management and Support System Limited Nepal).

Further problems at the MOH include the drift of personnel to the private sector. All current project implementations have NGO participation and for this reason UNICEF is currently setting up umbrella organisations by districts. Among donors there is competition for the "good NGOs".

UNICEF describes their relations with the Ministry of Housing and Physical Planning as good while Finland's

FINIDA has recently diverted all its projects from this ministry to the Ministry of Local Development.

Relations with the Planning Commission

Donors agree that the capacity of Nepalese planners is very low but describe the people working in the Planning Commission as very conscientious. UNICEF has been sponsoring the Nepal Multiple Indicator Surveillance Project which provides indicators for health and nutrition. They have asked the Planning Commission to take over this project and the commission is in the process of doing so.

There are today three general forms of participation in the planning process in Nepal:

- the form described above where a leader or a minister orders participation;
- the sitting allowance participation, where ministerial employees are paid to be present. General fees are now Rs 300–400 per person or a flat rate of Rs 50,000 per ministry (this form is very common in the health sector); and
- the form described below, namely participation where local pressure groups are formed (real participation).

Ministry of Finance (MOF)

The Ministry of Finance is a super-ministry which provides financing to the other ministries. Donors prefer to work directly with line ministries but large amounts need to be channelled through the MOF. If you want to finance a local training centre, for example (as UNICEF often does), the channel of finance should be as per Figure 16 (overleaf). This process is very slow and thus donors have to advance substantial amounts for ongoing activities. Furthermore, although the Ministry of Finance audits donors' accounts if their money has been channelled

Figure 16: The channel of finance to a local training centre

through the Ministry to the recipient organisation, accounting is behind by an average of three years. However, if donors fund the recipient organisation directly, they have to do their own auditing.

Sustainability

Projects that have been taken over by the Nepalese government often incur problems of sustainability. When donors stop their support, projects are known to end and sometimes actually disappear. As no political or economic reward may be expected, employees are often transferred to more interesting ventures.

NGOS AND DEVELOPMENT AID

Whereas material collected from international organisations has been incorporated in the text, material pertaining to NGOs has only been touched on sporadically, even though these can be a major conduit for aid funds to be channelled to Nepal (e.g., see Table 12 opposite).

Table 12: Recent Norwegian aid to Nepal channelled through Norwegian NGOs

NGO	Amount (NOK)
Den Norske Advokatforening	710,550
Norsk Misjonsråds Bistandsnemnd	1,758,00
CARE Norge	1,074,000
Den Norske Tibetmisjon	190,732
Funksjonshemmedes Bistandsstiftelse	2,339,000
Utviklingsfondet	276,000
Kirkens Nødhjelp	3,183,000
Nasjonalforeningen for Folkehelsa	67,840
Norsk Lærerlag	401,998
Redd Barna	6,321,000
Total	**16,322,120**

Source: NORAD, 1996.

However, the following sections include information gained in interviews with two Norwegian organisations that are both active in Nepal: Redd Barna (Save the Children) and Norwegian Church Aid (Kirkens Nødhjelp, KN). Finally, due to its size and importance, the United Mission to Nepal is also discussed.

Norwegian Church Aid

Norwegian Church Aid (KN) has run eye hospitals in Nepal for many years, as well as a rural development project. Currently they are delegating the operational side of their involvement in Nepal to other NGOs (LWS) and to national trusts (NJS). No Norwegians are currently working for KN in Nepal, although KN's eye hospitals have been a major success story for Norwegian aid (see also page 108 above).

Redd Barna

Redd Barna, on the other hand, has 2 Norwegian employees in Kathmandu and 160 local employees. Like KN, they are basically working in the health sector and are pursuing their development targets in a professional way.

United Mission to Nepal

Lastly, Tibetmisjonen's involvement in Nepal through the United Mission to Nepal (UMN) has been described in detail in the chapter on energy (see especially page 34 onwards). We have recommended that a separate study of the UMN be carried out due to the vast involvement and experience accumulated by this organisation. Generally, the UMN is regarded as being one of the NGOs with the longest standing commitment in Nepal. Today it is also the largest. It is probable that Norwegian donors could benefit greatly in terms of "cost-benefit" by channelling funds through the UMN since much of the human involvement is voluntary. Furthermore, the accumulation of knowledge which has been acquired by UMN personnel is a "capital source" which is invaluable to donors.

Views of Political Parties on Development in These Sectors

In this chapter we reproduce data gathered from interviews with the main Nepalese political parties on themes relevant to proposed Norwegian aid. We have included this section because the government today is very fragile (see Figure 17) and policy could well differ if, say, the Communists took over. This could affect investments in the energy sector especially but also in all other sectors. Regarding health and education, a more decentralised approach could be expected, and in the field of human rights there would probably be more focus on the down trodden and poor. Issues such as women's ownership rights would also be pursued with greater vigour.

COMMUNIST PARTY OF NEPAL (UML)

The Communist Party of Nepal (United Marxist-Leninist) – commonly known as the UML – consists of many factions of different communist groups. Despite the loss of its leader, Bandari (in a possibly non-accidental car crash?), the party won the election in 1995 under Man Mohan Adikari. It held power for only 9 months,

Figure 17: Balance of power in the current Nepali parliament

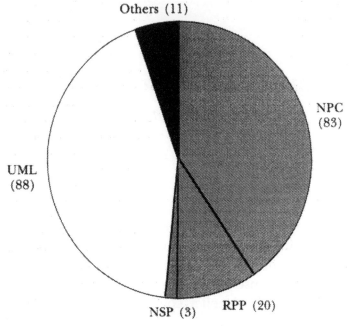

Notes: (1) Government parties shaded gray
(2) Number of seats held in brackets
(3) NSP = Nepal Sadbhavana Party

being a minority government. Today Adikari's ill-health keeps him out of the political arena and a new generation of leaders is emerging. The UML is believed capable of winning an election should one be held today.

The UML claims to be different from all other communist parties in the world. It has no formal ties with China or Russia and its slogan is "we support what the people want". Since the Nepali people are in favour of the king, a constitutional monarchy is also part of UML policy.

The Power Sector

The UML's policy is to support small- and medium-sized hydroelectric projects. It is not opposed to large-scale projects in principle but objects to large dams for environmental and ecological reasons.

The most pressing polictical issue today – one that could even lead to a change in government – relates to the use of rivers that run from Nepal to India. The UML opposes the Mahakali Treaty that has been concluded with India concerning water rights because it considers that, as it stands, the treaty does not give equal access to resources. Parliament is to vote on the treaty which will require a three quarters majority. The UML is hoping to topple the government over this issue.

The Human Rights Sector

The UML claims to have been in the forefront of establishing human rights in Nepal. In 1990 the UML formed part of the popular democracy movement and helped to create FORFUR (the Forum for Human Rights), the first human rights organisation in Nepal. The UML was also involved in the establishment by the General Federation of Nepalese Trade Unions of the Bonded Labour Forum to fight against all forms of slavery in the country.

While the UML were in power, they proposed that a human rights commission be created in Nepal. This, however, was voted down in Parliament by the Congress Party. A compensation bill for those abused through slavery was also drawn up but again failed to win support from the Congress Party. A bill concerning property rights (the Equal Rights Bill) is currently being debated in Parliament. This proposes granting women the right to own land in Nepal for the first time. The UML supports the bill, the Congress Party is divided over the issue, and the Royalist Party is so far undecided (some claim that the bill could lead to anarchy). It is unlikely that such a bill will be passed by the present Parliament since it is at odds with the tradition of women marrying out of the family. The Nepalese do not consider it worthwhile spending money on women who are destined to leave the family, unlike male children who will stay in the family and care for its aged members.

The UML is currently expecting a mid-term poll and has therefore suggested an identity card project. This scheme has the support of DANIDA but not, however, the approval of the governing Congress Party. The UML also supports the Voters Education Programme, which was started by INSEC, but denies that there has been any INSEC infiltration.

The UML were responsible for providing human rights education through Radio Nepal. They claim that under their leadership no censorship was applied, although this is not the case today under the leadership of the Congress Party.

Parliament has recently passed several laws on human rights (bonded labour, women's rights, etc.) but it lacks a means of enforcement. For instance the law against trafficking in women is infringed by the sale of women to brothels.

The Education Sector

Before the UML came to power (during 1994–95), free education was only available up to lower secondary level (grade 7). Today, thanks to the support of the UML, there is free education up to high school level (grade 10).

The UML intends to establish a primary school in all Nepali villages, employing a minimum of 3 teachers. They also advocate that all teachers should be educated to at least high school level. The party strongly supports vocational training and a vocational training centre is proposed for all the 14 zones of Nepal.

The Health Sector

The UML's "Build Your Village Yourselves" (BOVO) programme brought a form of decentralised democracy to the countryside. This programme extended health services throughout the country. The UML's current policy favours auxilary health workers and midwives over doctors, intermediary health personnel being seen as the most effective way of providing health care to rural districts. The party also says that doctors should be rewarded with specialisation grants if they promise to practise in the countryside. The privatisation of medical practices and hospitals is not encouraged.

The UML is more concerned with the well-being of the poor than in attracting increased numbers of supporters at election time. Therefore family planning is encouraged. Social welfare for the elderly is also regarded as important.

Suggestions for Norwegian Cooperation

In terms of the high chance of a UML return to power, priority should first be given to the health sector, then to human rights. Government employees, including the police, should be educated in human rights issues. Today 60 per cent of total government spending is provided by foreign aid. It is essential therefore that such aid reaches the poor.

NEPAL CONGRESS PARTY

The Nepal Congress Party (NCP) was established as the first national party and led the democracy movement in the 1950s. The party was then led by the legendary B.P. Koirala. Now it is run by his younger brother, G. P. Koirala. A split in the party over allegience to G.P. Koirala and a rival leader, Ganesh Man Singh, led to the party's defeat in the 1995 elections. Today the NCP heads a coalition government with the RPP (see page 130 below).

Decentralisation

Since central bureaucracy does not appear to function well in Nepal, the NCP is strongly in favour of decentralisation. During its nine months in power, the communist UML government started to fund local development areas directly. Such VDCs were previously called *panchayats*, which the NCP claim to have always focused on. During the first Congress government, 70 per cent of government spending was in rural areas and more than 1,000 primary schools were opened. One in three villages had village health posts.

The NCP criticised the UML's decentralised "Build Your Village Yourselves" programme as 50 per cent of direct VDC grants were unused and infrastructural investments such as roads were destroyed by the monsoon. However, the NCP government continues to provide technical support to the VDCs and allow them to levy their own taxes (previously only 20 per cent of these were allowed to be used within the VDC). Furthermore, the NCP government provides project-based support directly to each VDC.

The Education Sector

The NCP government disagrees with the UML's policy of emphasising vocational training and the "10+2" education programme. It feels that too much funding is tied up in the university structure (Tribhuwan University is administered by communists who refuse to resign and the present coalition government has encountered problems with students and teachers there). The NCP encourages private schools and universities and wants to raise all university fees.

The Health Sector

All parties share basically the same policy on health. However, the NCP places more emphasis on drinking water and sanitation since 60 per cent of all diseases are spread by unclean water resources. Health education through mass communication and other media is also a priority for the NCP.

The Human Rights Sector

The NCP is split over its views on the women's ownership bill currently under discussion in Parliament. Some MPs maintain that culture should be respected and property inheritance should be allocated according to the wishes of the parents.

The Power Sector

The NCP favours the use of hydroelectricity. Today only 250 MW have been developed out of a possible 65,000 MW. However, better use of all fuel resources is being encouraged.

RASHTRIYA PRAJANTRA PARTY

The Rashtriya Prajantra Party (RPP) has its roots among members of the earlier *Panchayat* movement. This movement, headed by the King, ruled Nepal from 1951 until the 1990 democratic revolution. Today, the RPP claims that it no longer supports autocracy and is a national democratic party. During the last election it received approximately 20 per cent of votes. The RPP is now a member of the government coalition together with the Congress Party.

The Power Sector

The RPP emphasises that any development in Nepal is dependent on the main resource of hydroelectricity. It claims that India takes too large a share and dictates prices. Accordingly, the RPP advocates an equal Mahakali Treaty with India in order to develop Nepal. This position is in contrast with that of the UML; the RPP is against development that needs poverty as a framework for social mobilisation.

The Education Sector

The RPP recognises that education is central to all development. However, it supports more emphasis on vocational training. The RPP's plan for education includes the provision of ordinary schools up to the eighth grade with the ninth and tenth grades being vocational. It points out that, while unemployment is on the increase in Nepal, locally there are still skills shortages – for instance, barbers and carpenters are being recruited from India.

The Health Sector

The party states that privatisation of the health sector should continue in the cities but state incentives should be provided in rural areas in recognition of the semi-feudal situation which still exists there. The RPP believes that primary health care is essential through the VDC health posts, and that district and regional hospitals are also desirable. Each electoral constituency should have a health centre with 5–10 beds. The RPP also supported the new health bill recently passed by the upper house of Parliament which requires doctors to serve in rural areas for a year (270 days of actual residence).

The RPP supports the building of private hospitals such as the one established in Pathan by the UMN. It believes, however, that democracy does not mean that people can establish enterprises unchecked; laws are needed to regulate private and public health services.

The Human Rights Sector

Although the observation of human rights is essential, the establishment of a human rights committee must be delayed as the issue has become politicised with the Left making the human rights issue part of their wider political agenda. The RPP is divided on the equal rights bill for women regarding ownership of land. It states that most of the national and international NGOs are controlled by pro-UML forces and the communists benefit from this. The RPP maintains that, in order to provide impartial elections, all border crossings should be recorded and voters should have registration cards. According to the RPP, the communists do not support identity cards as these will prevent (pro-UML) voters from voting more than once; this, they say, happened at the university which is now run by pro-UML officials.

General Conclusions and Remarks

Below is a summary of the conclusions contained in the chapters dealing with energy, human rights, education and health issues. Please refer to the full text of these chapters for a better understanding of our reasoning.

THE ENERGY SECTOR

Since hydropower is one of Nepal's few natural resources which are abundantly available and is of central importance for the development of the country, this resource should be exploited. In the process, however, the expertise and the capacity of the Nepalese themselves to handle this development has to be in focus. To a large extent this strategy has already been employed and here it can be argued that on the whole the Norwegian engagement in the Nepalese energy sector has been fairly successful.

Steps have been made first to assist in the creation of a training centre and later the initiative has been taken to create a number of Nepalese companies which through training and practice can build up expertise in various aspects of hydropower development. Initially, small projects were undertaken to build up basic experience and know-how but more recently the projects have grown in size and complexity in line with the capacity of the Nepalese companies to handle construction with a minimum of foreign assistance. However, large and complex projects like Khimti Khola are too big to be financed and implemented solely with donor money and using local competence.

Alternatively, the development of many smaller plants may open up other new and exciting possibilities. These can be adapted to local conditions and be vital to support and initiate further regional and local development. Given the great political uncertainty as well as economic and technical complexities connected with the development of large hydropower plants, there can be no doubt that the Norwegian contribution should preferably be weighted towards development of small- and maybe medium-sized plants, and here the technological know-how of Norwegian companies could play a decisive role. Another area where there is scope for input is in the field of micro-hydropower which when installed in remote, roadless areas may act as a catalyst for the local economy, especially if it is done in conjunction with rural development.

THE HUMAN RIGHTS SECTOR

Although public democratic institutions and the civil rights situation do not seem to have improved substantially over the last few years, political rights are much developed and this may pave the way for further changes. A possible combination of DANIDA and USAID in electoral issues would, however, be useful. While there is a tendency towards political abuse in the NGO sector, NGOs as a whole are useful in channelling aid to many organisations. Another method of furthering democracy would be to support the peaceful understanding of ethnic diversity. Any such efforts, however, would need to be co-ordinated between a multitude of donors.

THE EDUCATION SECTOR

Even if Norway does not wish to become a large-scale implementor in the educational sector in Nepal, it would still be prudent to invest in the BPEP structure. Furthermore, if other large-scale donors invest in the "10+2" strategy, this is likely to have a big impact on the quality of teaching in the future. However, before any investment can be made in the "10+2" alternative, the Nepalese government must specify its monetary policy regarding this new endeavour. In addition, a system for direct financing of the new "10+2" private and public institutions must be considered.

The largest challenge facing Nepal in the near future is not the provision of education *per se* (although there are serious imbalances between especially secondary schools in the public and private sectors, and between those close to and those remote from Kathmandu). Rather, the largest challenge is the provision of occupational training that in turn can help to alleviate unemployment. There is, then, a need to strengthen vocational training. A secondary vocational training effort within high schools is currently being developed as an alternative to "10+2". This may become an interesting and important development arena.

THE HEALTH SECTOR

The Health sector in Nepal is badly organised, over-bureaucratic and difficult to work with. Its absorption capacity of foreign aid is very low. Due to donor difficulties working with government ministries, short-term project-orientated aid rather than a long-term programme approach should probably be favoured, with specific activities that can be closely monitored at each step the first priority. The development of a similar donor structure to that used in the Ministry of Education may be the solution in the short run; direct financing is another option. The possibility of co-financing with bilateral donors should also be pursued and it is also important to develop relationships with international NGOs such as UNICEF and WHO.

Appendix 1

Norsk Resymé

ENERGISEKTOREN I NEPAL

I dag utnytter Nepal først og fremst skogene sine for å dekke sitt energibehov (86%), men landet importerer også en hel del fossilt brensel. Vannkraften utgjør bare 1% av det totale energiforbruk. Her er imidlertid potensialet enormt. Det er beregnet at den totale mengden utnyttbar vannkraft ligger et sted i størrelsesorden 83.000 MW og av dette er cirka en tredjedel mulig å eksportere kommersielt. Hittil er bare cirka 250 MW bygd ut. Nepal satser i dag store ressurser på å bygge ut energisektoren og i den siste femårsplanen har 20,9% av den totale budsjettallokeringen blitt avsatt til dette formålet. Av disse ressursene går 99% til vannkraft, fortrinnsvis til store prosjekter. Ved siden av vannkraft har biogass, vind og solenergi også blitt ført frem som alternativer, og særlig da med tanke på avsidesliggende områder.

Det norske engasjementet i den nepalske energisektoren kan spores tilbake til 1958 da den norske elektroingeniøren, Odd Hofftun, ble engasjert av United Mission to Nepal (UMN). Gjennom UMN har et teknisk institutt som formidler såvel teoretisk som praktisk

trening blitt bygget opp i Butwal. UMN har vært
drivkraften i oppbyggingen av private selskaper, Butwal
Power Company og Himal Hydro, som bygger opp og
ivaretar nepalesisk ekspertise innen vannsektoren.
Allerede i 1966 påbegynte man konstruksjonen av det
første 1 MW-prosjektet og flere andre har siden fulgt
etter. For inneværende år er et relativt stort, 60 MW-
anlegg, Khimti Khola, under implementering. I dette
arbeidet har flere norske bedrifter, Statkraft Anlegg,
Kværner og ABB blitt engasjert og gått inn med såvel
kapital som ekspertise. Siden 1993 har Norge gjennom
ekspertise fra Norges Vassdrags- og Energiverk også
bidratt til utviklingen av et lovverk som skal regulere
utviklingen og anvendelsen av vannressurser. To lover,
en "Water Use Act" og en "Electricity Law" har blitt
skrevet.

Den nepalesiske administrasjonen innen vannsektoren er delt opp i fire regjeringsorgan hvor Ministry
of Water Resources (MWR) er det departement som
har det overordnede ansvar for utviklingen. Under seg
har MWR etablert et Electricity Development Centre
som skal ha ansvaret for at vannkraftprosjekter gjennomføres på en smidig måte. Dessuten finnes Water and
Energy Commission som er rådgivere til HMG for en
koordinert utvikling av vann og energiressurser. Til
slutt finnes Nepal Electricity Authority (NEA) som er
satt til å regulere produksjon, overføring og distribusjon
av elektrisitet. Til tross for at hver og en av disse fire
organene har sine egne vel definerte oppgaver, så er
det i virkeligheten slik at de overlapper hverandre og
noen ganger har de til og med gitt motstridende
opplysninger som har resultert i stor og tilbakevendende
forvirring.

NEA er den viktigste institusjonen når det gjelder
utvikling av vannkraft. De har identifisert og prosjektert

et antall mulige vannkraftverk. De fleste av disse er over
100 MW men en del er av mellomstørrelsen 30–70 MW.
Til utviklingen av de store kraftverkene ønsker regjeringen støtte fra ulike långivere som ADB og WB
mens man for de små og mellomstore oppfordrer den
private sektor til å medvirke. Mens NEA er mest
interessert i å utvikle de store kraftverkene, så foreligger
det også stor interesse for å utvikle små kraftverk spredd
over hele landet. Disse skal kunne bli økonomisk
konkurransedyktige og til og med gi viktige bidrag til
en uavhengig utvikling for distriktene.

Den pågående og planlagte utbyggingen av store
vannkraftverk har voldt store politiske kontroverser i
Nepal. Dette gjaldt særskilt det planlagte Verdens-
bankstøttede Arun III-prosjektet, som var planlagt til
402 MW. I 1993–94 pågikk en intensiv debatt hvor
prosjektet og dets vilkår ble sterkt kritisert. Da NC-
regjeringen falt i desember 1994 og ble erstattet av en
CPN-UML regjering, ble det stilt nye vilkår og Verdensbanken besluttet i august 1995 å ikke gjennomføre
prosjektet. De trakk tilbake 700 millioner dollar men
lovet 150 millioner dollar i støtte til mindre kraft-
utbygginger. Nylig har en annen vannkraftutbygging i
Makahali skapt nye konflikter. Det utløsende denne
gangen var en avtale mellom India og Nepal som skulle
regulere hvordan vannressursene i elvene skulle fordeles.
NC som nå sitter i regjeringsposisjon støttet avtalen,
mens CPN-UML truet med å stemme imot. 22 september
1996 ble likevel forslaget ratifisert med minst mulig
majoritet (1 stemme). Nepal er helt avhengig av India
for å ha mulighet til å eksportere eventuelt overskuddsenergi. Det indiske energimarkedet er imidlertid høyt
subsidiert, og Nepal må derfor få i stand en avtale som
gir landet rett til å selge sin overskuddsenergi til
verdensmarkedspris og ikke til Indias subsidierte nivå.

Dersom en slik avtale ikke kommer i stand blir det politisk umulig for NC å forsvare videre satsning i stor skala. Vannutbyggingsprosjekter, store såvel som små, medfører nødvendigvis visse miljømessige og sosiale påvirkninger. Innen et prosjekt blir igangsatt er det nødvendig at økonomisk kompensasjon diskuteres og besluttes. For eksempel bør avtaler om en vanndeling og tilretteleggelsen for å sikre migrasjon av fisk tas opp. I denne sammenheng er det viktig at den lokale befolkningen gis en mulighet til aktivt å delta i beslutningsprosessen og ikke bare, som hittil oftest har skjedd, blir informert etter at beslutningen er tatt. Sett i et videre perspektiv har en vannkraftutbygging mange positive miljømessige sider idet den reduserer bruk av andre energikilder. Den nåværende overutnyttingen av skogressursene, først og fremst til brensel, er på god veg til å resultere i en økologisk katastrofe. Vannreguleringen i Nepal kan til og med bidra til å minske skadevirkningene av oversvømningskatastrofene som regelmessig finner sted på sletteområdene nord i India og Bangladesh der elvene har sitt utløp.

Konklusjon

Vannkraft er en av få nepalesiske naturressurser som er fornybare og tilgjengelige. Utnyttelse av denne ressursen er svært viktig for landets fremtidige utviklingsmuligheter. I denne sammenhengen er det av avgjørende betydning at nepalesernes egen kapasitet er bygget ut og vedlikeholdt, og drift av vannkraftverk må stilles i fokus. Modellen for kompetanseoverføring som er bygget opp av UMN gjennom deres snart 40-årige virksomhet innen sektoren har lykkes godt og er vel egnet til å bygges videre på. Ved å først konsentrere seg om små og mindre kompliserte prosjekter, har man suksessivt opparbeidet grunnleggende erfaring og know-how. De store prosjektene som ble planlagt av NEA og skulle gjennomføres med støtte fra Verdensbanken og/eller andre multinasjonale bistandsgivere er altfor store, teknisk komplisert og politisk kontroversielle til å fungere som et ledd i en gradvis kompetanseoppbygging.

En satsning på små og muligens også i en viss utstrekning mellomstore prosjekter har derimot helt andre muligheter til å bestå og til og med gi avgjørende bidrag til landets utvikling. I utviklingen av slike prosjekt kan norske bedrifter som Statkraft Anlegg, Kværner og ABB få stor innflytelse og aktivt bidra til overføring av kunnskap. Til og med i spørsmål om de svært små mikrokraftverkene som kan bygges ut i avsidesliggende, veiløse områder har Norge mulighet til å gjøre en avgjørende innsats. Kombinert med satsning på landsby-utvikling har de forskjellige mikrokraftverk muligheten til å fungere som katalysator for videre utviklings-initiativ i økonomisk svake områder.

UTDANNELSE

- Inntil 1950 var utdannelse bare tilgjengelig for de kongelige og utvalgte høykaste folk i Nepal.

- 1971 standardisering av tekstbøker og curriculum for grunnskolen.

- 1990 underskriving av erklæringen fra Bangkoks verdenskonferanse om utdannelse.

Man får den første nasjonale utdannelsesplan: Øke antallet av de som går på grunnskole fra 64 % til 100%, særlig blant kvinner hvor deltagelsen var 31%. Antallet av de som "fullfører" grunnskolen skulle også økes fra 27 til 70% de neste 10 år.

- Den overordnede strategi siden 1990 er primært å satse på grunnskolen ved å
  1) øke tilgangen til skoler (dvs. bygge flere), og
  2) øke kvaliteten (dvs. forbedre lærekreftene og få bedre curriculum og tekstbøker.
- Planen fra den åttende 5-årsplanen (til 1997) er at 90% av alle barn skal få tilgang til grunnskolen. innen 1997. Her skilles meget på *tilgang* og *obligatorisk krav.* Dette er tilfelle fordi man ikke har et program for å gi barna mat på skolen etc., samt subsidiere fattige familier som trenger barnas arbeidsinnsats. Norske NGOer som Antislaveriselskapet, Redd Barna, og Tibetmisjonen innen UMN arbeider med egne støtteverdige problematikker.
- Tall: Man har i dag omkring 22.000 grunnskoler, med 3,2 millioner elever, og 85.000 lærere, hvorav bare 50.000 har SLC eksamen. Det er ca 95 elever pr lærer, og det vil ta 60 år å komme ajour.

Finans

MOE har det største budsjett av alle departementer i Nepal. De får 13%, eller 57,6 billioner Rps. (sammenlignet med helsedep. som får 6%). 2/3 deler av budsjettet er lønninger som styres av MOE og 1/3 del er prosjektpenger fra internasjonale donorer. Også lån inverteres i denne sektoren.

Utdannelsessystemet

Utdannelsessystemet er delt i tre med primary, secondary og høyere utdannelse. Det er 5 år i hvert av de to første trinnene, med en offentlig eksamen kaldt SLC (School Learning Certificate) etter 10 år. Man vil nå *legge til to år i en spesielt yrkesrettet universitet/videregående utdannelse* kalt 10+2. Dette for å frigjøre ressurser fra universitetet og heve nivå på *sekundærutdannelse.* Man regner med at antall studieplasser på universitet kan reduseres med ca 67%.

Universitetssystemet fungerer dårlig, med et stort sentralt universitet oppkalt etter den gamle kong Tribhuvan, og med 150.000 registrerte studenter og 61 "campuses". Private universitet og skoler er med stor fart på vei inn i utdannelsessystemet. 80% av dem som tar SLC er nå fra private skoler.

Ministry of Education (MOE) og den alternative donorstruktur.

Man er generelt enige om at kapasiteten til MOH er lav, og at man ikke kan diskutere faglig med personalet der. Nå har man laget et "Higher Education Board" og en "Institute of Education" for å bøte på dette, men donorer har funnet det formålstjenlig å bygge opp en "alternativ"/repliserende struktur. Her har man skapt et stort *paraplyprogram for hvert nivå* av utdannelsene og flere donorer er inne i de fleste nivåer. (Se fig. i rapport. Store donorer er UNDP; ADB; ODA; DANIDA; UNICEF og JICA).

BPEP

Dette prosjektet ble startet i 1991 samtidig som den første "Master Plan of Primary Education 1991–2001)". Totalt budsjett over 10 år har vært på 118,5 millioner dollar.

Det er det største og mest vellykkede utdannelsesprosjekt i Nepal, men har fullstendig tatt over funksjoner fra MOE. Donorene koordinerer seg imellom; DANIDA (leder/oppbygger Resource Centers pr. VDC, utdannelse av kvinner), UNICEF (tekstbok og curriculum utvikling, non-formal education), JICA (material for skolebygging, sement, tak etc. JICA (Japan) er ellers største donor i Nepal, mest i "hardware").

Dette prosjektets første fase gikk ut i år og man dekket 40 av Nepals distrikter. Andre fase vil dekke de resterende 35 distriktene.

Higher Education School Project (10+2)

Mål for den niende 5-årsplan er at sekundærnivået i utdannelsen skal være totalfinansiert. I dag er paradoksalt nok universitetet fritt, men sekundærnivået må eleven selv betale. Som et videre ledd vil en overføre penger og lærere fra universitetsstrukturen til en utvidet sekundærutdannlese. Denne utvides med to år, samtidig som den blir mer yrkesrettet. Private og offentlige strukturer samarbeider her. En trenger likevel donorpenger for å få økonomien, insentivene til å fungere. Det bygges nytt og lærere må "lures" over ved høyere lønn etc. ADB har utviklet tekstbøker, programmet fungerer, men bør økes. Ingen store donorer er inne nå.

Andre prosjekter

For interessante lærerutviklingsprosjekter, se kapitel om PEDP i rapporten.

Konklusjon

Om UD ikke selv ønsker å være prosjektimplementerende i noe større grad, er BPEP prosjektet i fase 2 det alternativet som stikker seg fram. Dette må i så fall koordineres med DANIDA. Hva gjøres for å styrke MOE? Hvordan kan man få direkte finansiering av BPEP komponenter lokalt? En utredning med NGO deltagelse bør gjøres. Redd Barna og UMN bør kunne utføre dette i fellesskap. Ellers bør alle NGO alternativer innen utdannelse støttes idet de når spesielle grupper (barn, slaver etc) og drives godt. En utredning av UMNs rolle innen sektoren fra 1950 og framover kan kaste lys over norske pionerer og videreføre deres innsats.

Et annet alternativ er å støtte opp under 10+2 prosjektet. Dette vil skape *lærere* til den grunnskolen som nå blir bygget ut. Dette vil trolig få større virkning pr. norsk krone, og man vil sette sine spor i utdannelsessektoren. Spørsmålet her er hvordan MOE kan organisere den finansielle strukturen. Kan en støtte 10+2 skoler direkte uten å gå gjennom MOE? Kan et slikt alternativ koordineres med andre donorer?

HELSE

Møgedal-rapporten (Mars 1996)

Denne fyldige og anbefalelsesverdige rapporten konkluderer:

- Helsetjenesten i Nepal er i nedgang. Bare ca 20 % av landets befolkning har tilgang til primærhelsetjenester
- Lik tilgang og lik fordeling er hovedproblemer. Økonomien er dårlig styrt og underfinansiert. Man bør tenke i nye baner, ikke bare øke volumet av bistand.
- Privatisering foregår raskt, men bare i urbane sentra. Regjeringen bør regulere mellom private og offentlige tilbud.
- Man bør bygge videre på det som frivillige og internasjonale organisasjoner gjør i dag.

Anbefalinger er:

a) bruke multi-/bilaterale kanaler i inneværende år
b) støtte til første "referal unit" nivå (Primary Health Centers, PHC) som nå etableres på valgkrets basis, eller alternativt distriktshospitalsnivå

Sigrun Møgedal anbefaler ellers å bygge ut styringskapasitet og ledelse i Ministry of Health (MOH), gitt at man overveier regulær støtte til Departementet og United Mission in Nepals sykehus i Kathmandu.

Denne rapporten støtter hennes konklusjoner a) og b), men vi mener ellers at MOHs absorberingskapsitet bør økes før et samarbeide skal finne sted. MOH blir per i dag sett på som det mest tungrodde og vanskeligste av alle de departement man kan arbeide med i landet.

Finansieringsstruktur

MOH mottok ca 3,5 billioner Rps. som utgjør ca 6% av statsbudsjettet for 1996/7. I 1992/3 klarte man ikke å bruke mer enn ca. 76% av pengene og denne trenden er lik i dag. Man fikk ikke brukt mer enn ca 50% av det som var lovet av bistandspenger (disbursment) fra 1980 til 1992, og det var en uoverensstemmelse mellom forbruk og budsjettering i samme tidsrom på fra ca. 19% til 719%. Utfra dette ser en et sprik mellom planlegging og gjennomføring.

Sektoren mottok i 1994/5 ca 400 millioner dollar i utenlandsstøtte, hvorav kun 30 millioner i lån.

Planleggingskapasitet, ledelse og styring

Planleggingskapasitet ser ut til å være bedre enn evnen til å følge planene. Personal omskiftes stadig, leger er ikke på post om de ikke er stasjonert i Kathmandu-dalen, og kaste hierarkiske relasjoner, samt parti relasjoner motvirker oppbygning av moderne strukturer. Man betaler også lite til de som reiser utenfor Kathmandu-dalen. Per diem er ca 10 kr. dagen.

Mange har prøvet å øke MOH planleggingskapsitet, (German Aid, WB, USAID, UNFPA, ADB, UNICEF). Det siste er UNICEFs Multiple Indicator Surveillance Strategy, men det har vist seg vanskelig på den ene siden å få de planleggende myndigheter til å ta over, og på den andre siden å få tilstrekkelig data fordi det ikke

finnes personal i store deler av landsby-Nepal. Man får
derfor ikke innrapportert tilstrekkelig.

Oppbygging av den regionale helsetjeneste
Figuren under (del av MOH figur i rapporten – se side 99)
illustrerer hvordan den lokal helsetjenesten er bygget opp.

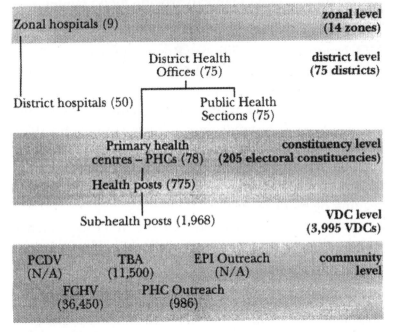

Man hadde tidligere en satsning på Health posts (HP)
og Zonal hospitals (fram til 1990) men man har av
politiske grunner nå lagt til to nivåer, et over og et
under Health post -nivå. Over HP nivået har en fått de
såkalte Primary health centres (PHC). Dette er det
første nivået hvor en nå vil ha inn leger. Det finnes dog
District hospitals uten leger også i dag. PHC-nivået er
viktig fordi dette fungerer per valgkrets. Valgkretsene i
Nepal er forskjellige fra kommune- og fylkesgrenser.
    Det andre nivået er Sub-health posts (SHP). Dette
nivåer er viktig siden det faller sammen med VDC

(Pancahyat-nivået) i den nye desentraliserte nepalesiske struktur. Kommunistene begynte med "block grant" kalt "bygg din egen landsby" i 1994 (med 300.000 Rps pr. VDC, og den nåværende samlingsregjeringen har fortsatt dette fordi det ble meget populært blant velgerne. Helsestasjoner og lokale veibygg fikk nå preferanse.

Regjeringens mål

Man satser primært i den ny desentraliserte helseplanen (8. og 9. femårsplan) på primærhelsetjeneste. Her vil man bygge 20 nye PHC og 600 nye SHP innen utgangen av 1996. Man har fått 26 millioner US dollar som soft loan fra Verdenbanken for å gjennomføre dette.

Delmål (barnedødelighet, fertilitet, barseldødelighet, livslengde, etc.) og metoder (vaksinering, familie planlegging, malaria spraying, hygiene osv.) for å nå disse (se i hovedrapporten).

Antall nye hospital skyter fart innen både det private (stort sett Kathmandu) og det offentlige (Pokhara, Kathmandu og Baratpur (kreftsykehus)).

Man kan ikke skaffe personal til den strukturen som er bygget opp med SHP og PHC. Ayavedic dvs. tradisjonelt hindu-trent personell dominerer. Dog er halvparten av befolkningen nå Buddhister og de ser på denne trenden som en sanskritisering. Dvs. "hindi-fisering" av landet.

Politikk og muligheter

Det er i dag umulig for noen av de politiske partier og gå bort fra desentraliseringstrenden innen helse. Dette fører til at man får mindre på den sektoren som til nå har fått mest, nemlig sykehus.

Bortsett fra de politiske mål som dette reflekterer i kampen om "grunnplanet" dvs 80% av Nepals befolkning (på landsbygda), finnes det også medisinske begrunnelser for dette:

Studier viser f. eks. at man kan redusere barnedødelighet med ca. 50% hvis man gir hygiene utdannelse
og viser hvordan man hanskes med lungebetennelse,
samt kompenserer for mangel på Vitamin A. Om man i
tillegg vaksinerer mot barnesykdommer og støtter opp
under globale programmer (malaria etc.) argumenteres
det med at man får mest ut av pengene brukt. Kan man
også få en fungerende befolkningsplanlegging gjennom
primærhelsetjenesten, vil dette få store innvirkninger i
Nepal. Alt dette er vel og bra, hvis man da ikke er så
uheldig å bli så syk at man trenger sykehus. Disse
fungerer nå dårlig og man satser lite utenom i den
private sektor på sykehusbygging.

Privatisering

To utviklingsmodeller som til dels utelukker hverandre
(idet de kan konkurrere om samme knappe ressurser)
er den offentlige og en private helsevisjon. Jeg fikk
innblikk i den private filosofi i intervju med nepalesiske forretningsmenn som i dag investerer i helse.

Det første spørsmålet for det private initiativ er:
Hvorfor investere i landsby prosjekter når likevel meste-
parten av nepalesere er på flyttefot til Kathmandu-
dalen? 80% bor på landsbygda i dag, men vi kan ikke
forvente at man får en annen utvikling enn man gjør i
andre land. Derfor vil organiseringen bare gå raskere
og raskere, og det gjelder derfor å gjøre seg klar til å
motta disse utfordringene. Legene og helsepersonell vil
likevel ikke reise ut på landsbygda, men vil gjerne ha
jobb i private bedrifter. Det er til i dag opprettet ca 100
gamlehjem i Kathmandu, idet hotell konverteres til slik
bruk. Private klinikker og sykehus spetter opp. Man vil
lage tilbud av første klasse for å tiltrekke seg pasienter
fra Nord India. (Uttar Pradesh). Disse må nå reise langt
syd i India fordi helsetjenester er dårlig utbygget i nord.

Minister Arjun Narasingh K.C. ser på denne utviklingen som positiv, men vil ikke ha "quango" strukturer. (Quasi Governmental Structures). Ingen donor-penger bør flyte til det private. Der finnes det nok av penger, er utsagnet. National Health Policy Strategy Plan (part 4.6), samt ESAP programmet (Enhanced Structural Adjustment Program) gjør det lett for business-mennene å operere i et uregulert marked. Med sine politiske kontakter og sine formuer, samt kaste- og regionale nettverk, kan de lett gå mot regulering av det private helsevesen. Man bør vurdere om man kan støtte opp under insentiv-programmer for å motvirke en flom av leger og personale til denne raskt ekspanderende sektoren.

Konklusjon

INGO sektoren og NGO sektoren bør være Norges primære artikulasjonskanaler innen helsesektoren. Man bør ikke gå inn med regulær budsjettstøtte til sektoren da administrasjonen er for normavvikende.

MENNESKERETTIGHETER

Demokrati og menneskerettigheter

Etter revolusjonen i 1990 har man i Nepal fått en markert bedring av en del menneskerettigheter. I dag diskuterer man politikk åpent, man kan danne politiske partier, og man har demokratiske valg (det siste med modifikasjoner, se under). Likevel er det mange ting som fortsetter som før. Man kan fortsatt bli fengslet uten lov og dom, torturert i fengslene, og man kan ha slaver slik man alltid har hatt. Tilgangen på rettigheter er meget avhengig av hvem du er.

Demokrati og valg

Formelt er Nepal nå et demokrati idet man har såkalte frie og uavhengige valg. Dog har innbyggerne i Nepal

ikke identitetspapirer, samtidig som man har under-
skrevet avtalen om en åpen grense med India. Under
valget i 1995, hvor Skar var med som inter-nasjonal
observatør, deltok anslagsvis (internasjonale kilder) ca.
en million indere. Parlamentarikere fra delstaten Uttar
Pradesh i India deltok i den nepalesiske valgkampen. De
uttalte seg til pressen og sa at deres etniske tilhørighet
(Yadav) var mer viktig for dem enn nasjonale grenser,
og at deres "supporters" kom fra begge land. Valget i
Nepal hadde også tilsnitt av "Ethnic block voting", dvs. at
grupper som stod i et motsetningsforhold til hverandre
valgte ulike partier for å profilere sin etniske tilhørighet.

Ellers ble valget i 95 gjennomført på bakgrunn av
manntallslister som var ti år gamle, og hvor identifiser-
ing gikk etter adresse, alder og navn. Da alle har klan-
navn i Nepal, og dermed har samme etternavn, regnet
man med (i den valgkrets jeg observerte) at kun
halvparten av de stemmeberettigede fikk stemme. Man
sa med en viss ironi at om man ikke hadde stemt innen
to timer etter at valgdørene åpnet, hadde andre gjort
det for deg. Jeg observerte at barn ned i 10-årsalderen
deltok, og at slaveeiere tok med seg sine familier inn i
stemmeavlukket. Andre holdt sine slaver hjemme
under strengt arbeid. Et parti (rojalistene) hadde kjøpt
opp 10.000 kvinnedrakter (sari) som de distribuerte
under valgkampen, og alkohol var ikke til å oppdrive
langs grensen til India, idet man fordelte denne for å få
stemmer. Vi hadde også tilfeller der urner ble "kapret"
av væpnede grupper. 10 personer ble rapportert døde
pga. valget. Til tross for store demonstrasjoner i
Kathmandu, var det lite om dette i pressen, og ikke noe
i TV. Som konklusjon kaller jeg demokratiet i Nepal for
et 20 % demokrati, hvor alle partier har like muligheter for
å korrumpere og hvor man under valg redistribuerer
goder til de fattige (for stemmer.)

Budsjett

Justisdepartementet er det departementet i Nepal som får minst av statsbudsjettet. For 1996/7 ble det tildelt 0.02 %. Dvs. 20 % av det kongen fikk som apanasje. Ministerposten er gitt til en eldre minoritetsforkjemper av lav kaste, og uten reel makt. Generelt kan man si at hans strategi har vært å få Nepal til å underskrive internasjonale traktater. Dette har vært meget vellykket (14 stk på 3 år), og danner ofte grunnlaget for det arbeidet som nepalesiske NGOer gjør i landet.

Nasjonale lover

Den nasjonale loven "Muluki Ain" av 1854, legger retningslinjene for Nepal som et hindu kongedømme. Denne loven ble ikke nevneverdig forandret i 1990. Kongen er fremdeles inkarnasjon av guden Vishnu, og alle etniske og sosiale grupper er fremdeles regulert ved lov. (Til sammenligning er dette ikke lovbestemt i India, (bare praksis), og Kongresspartiet er ikke så hindu dominert som i Nepal). Kongen har ikke lenger diktatorisk makt, men hans makt er større enn i andre land med konstitusjonelt monarki.

Hindu lov og nepalesiske tradisjoner er i konflikt ved flere tilfeller. Under nevnes noen som eksempel.

Kvinners rett til å eie fedres jord

Et av de mest interessante tema som i dag drøftes i Parlamentet er om kvinner skal ha rett til å arve jord etter sine fedre. Man har ratifisert internasjonale avtaler mot diskriminering, og en høyesterettsavgjørelse beordret Parlamentet til å ta opp saken. Mange mener at man her rokker ved noe av det mest grunnleggende i hindusamfunnet, nemlig at kvinner giftes ut av landsbyene der de er født. Om de da skal kunne eie jord i den landsbyen de kom fra vil hele fordelingssystemet forandres, hevdes det, og man forventer sosialt kaos. Alle partier, bortsett fra kommunistene som er for like rettigheter, er delt i dette spørsmålet. Få politikere vil bli gjenvalgt i sine valgkretser om de støttet internasjonale konvensjoner.

Slaveri

Hver første januar (Magh) i den nepalesiske kalender, kan man kjøpe mennesker i Nepal. Det vil si at man kan overta deres gjeld og få ansvaret for hele familier. Gjeld arves ikke ved lov i Nepal, men få vet om dette. Høykaster har i lang tid lagt under seg lavkaster i Nepals *tarari*, eller lavland. Spesielt etter at WHO fikk kontroll over malariaen der på 1950 tallet, ble rike jordbruksområder åpnet opp. Ca. 200.000 unge jenter er i dag solgt som prostituerte til India. Man anslår samlet antall slaver å kunne komme opp i ca 0.5 til 1 million. Også i byene og industrien kjøpes mennesker, bl. a. til teppeindustrien. Mange nepalesere sier at "bonded labour" ikke er slaveri, men ifølge FNs konvensjon er det definert som det. Ord som "paricipation" og deltagelse får en spesiell betydning når slaveeiere sender sine livegne til dugnad. "De er jo del av våre familier" har jeg hørt sagt.

Prostituerte som kommer hjem fra India har liten mulighet til å bli gjenintegret idet man går ut ifra at de har vært sammen med kasteløse. Derved utstøtes man.

Tortur og død

Det ble meldt om ca 100 tilfeller av tortur i nepalesiske fengsler i fjor, ifølge den Nepalesiske Menneskerettshåndboken (utgivelse støttet via NORAD). Man hadde innrapportert 25 tilfeller av dødsfall i fengslene, deriblant en mindreårig jente.

Etniske faktorer, religion og urbefolkninger

Et av de store konfliktpotensialene i dagens nepalesiske samfunn, er forholdet mellom hindu og buddhistisk tradisjon. Fram til folketellingen i 1991 trodde man at landet var 90% hindu. Det viste seg derimot at kun 49% svarte at de var hinduer. Til tross for at resultatene ikke ble offentliggjort, vet alle dette. Man har i dag en etnisk befolkning som delvis definerer seg som urbefolkning (*adivasi*), og som er større enn hindugrupperingen. Disse etniske gruppene dannet i 1990 en bevegelse som ble kalt Janajati (*jana* = flere, *jati* = kaste/gruppe). De uttalte klart at de ikke ville danne et politisk parti, og alle partiene fikk derved såkalte *janajati* representanter. Noe som resulterte i at partiene konkurrerte om etniske stemmer. I dag er alle partier enig om at man skal gi etniske minoriteter spesielle rettigheter. Nylig ble et etnisk universitet lansert i parlamentet, og NORAD ble mektig populær da de lanserte et prosjekt om et "nasjonalt fleretnisk kultursenter/Etnografisk Museum". Her skulle alle de etniske gruppe, de mektige som de små, vise fram det de var stolte av og derved gi hverandre en forståelse av nasjonal identitet og hvem" de andre" var i det nepalesiske samfunn. I dag er det ca 35 store etniske grupper (ca. 75 med stort og smått) i landet, og man snakker omkring 50 språk. Alle tiltak for fredelig nasjonal integrering er politisk populært.

AVSLUTTENDE KOMMENTARER OG KONKLUSJON

Det finnes i dag mange nasjonale NGOer som arbeider rundt menneskerettighetsspørsmål. Blant de mest kjente er FOFHUR, INHURED og INSEC. Alle er seriøse organisasjoner som vil kunne brukes som kanal for norsk bistand. Man bør helst spre støtten, idet hver og en oppfattes av de andre som også å spille en politisk rolle. DANIDA er den fjerde største donor i Nepal, og støtter opp under demokrati og desentralisering. Her burde det være et grunnlag for samarbeid, spesielt omkring arbeidet med identitetspapirer og valggjennomføring. Arbeid for de fattigste gruppene i landet gjøres best gjennom de norske NGOer som allerede er inne på dette feltet, f. eks.: Redd Barna og Antislaveriselskapet.

Appendix 2

Resource Book
of Foreign Aid Involvement Projects
under the Development Budget of the
Fiscal Year 1996–97

prepared by the
Nepalese Ministry of Finance
Foreign Aid Co-ordination Section

July 1996

Translation by Bhuvan Dahal
Anthropologist

Typesetting by Liz Bramsen
NIAS

Table of Contents

Summary of Budget – Division by Ministry

Aid No.	Name of Topics/Subtopics	His Majesty's Government of Nepal	Foreign Aid — Aid (Grant Assistance)					Foreign Aid — Loan assistance			Total Assistance	Grand Total
			Cash	To be paid	Direct Payment	Materials	Total	To be paid	Direct payment	Total		
35	Ministry of Finance	9000	119500	15000			134500				134500	143500
37	Ministry of Housing and Physical Planning	666257	128531	9110	114875	60710	313226	454229	72000	526229	839455	1505712
38	Ministry of Industry	1676			8408		8408	50380		50380	58788	60464
40	Ministry of Agriculture	685821	452083	45367	150450		647900	259802	2800	262602	910502	1596323
46	Ministry of Population and Environment	2626		11735			11735				11735	14111
47	Ministry of Water Resources	392307	74700	35500		110000	220200	1814038	439162	2253200	2473400	2865707
48	Ministry of Construction and Transportation	1302590	596500	42000	369618		1008118	838981	1284287	2123268	3131386	4433976
49	Ministry of Tourism and Civil Aviation	90261	49000		260000		309000	180436	168712	349148	658148	748409
55	Ministry of Land Reform and Management	2831			139397		139397				139397	142228
57	Ministry of Youth Sports and Culture	80	49000		5500		54500				54500	54580
59	Ministry of Forestry and Soil Conservation	72435	51108	24231	75574	8180	159093	77331		77331	236424	308859
65	Ministry of Education	445574	273092	62988	39148	300099	675327	1070548	296519	1367067	2042394	2487968
67	Ministry of Information and Communication	1150	10000	8000			18000				18000	19150
69	Ministry of Local Development	436485	57694	117158	114500	116300	405352	165416	30100	195516	600868	1037353
70	Ministry of Health	545460	201228	46602	485140	278336	1011306	505941	39484	545425	1556731	2102191
71	Ministry of Labour		1159				1159				1159	1159
72	Secretariat of the National Planning Commission	2781			12500		12500				12500	15281
87	Ministry of Finance—Investment (Internal Corporations)	494520	55000	30000	1187970		1272970	1094270	5011253	6105523	7378493	7873013
88	Ministry of Finance (Other Investments)							92817		92817	92817	92817
	TOTAL	5151604	2118295	447691	2963080	873625	6402691	6604189	7344317	13948506	20351197	25502801

Detailed Entries

Aid No.	Topic/Sub-topic	His Majesty's Government	Grant assistance: Cash	To be paid	Direct payment	Materials	Total	Loan no.	Loan: To be paid	Direct payment	Total	Total Assistance	Grand Total	Source of Aid
35.	MINISTRY OF FINANCE (BANKING SECTOR)	9000	119500	15000			134500					134500	143500	
35.4.301	Small Farmers Training and Institutional Dev. Aid		29500				29500					29500	29500	Germany
35.4.302	Gulmi Ardhakhachi Integrated Rural Development Programme			15000			15000					15000	15000	European Community for Co-operation
35.4.380	Bio Gas Production	9000	90000				90000					90000	99000	Germany – 75300 Netherlands – 14700
37	MINISTRY OF HOUSING AND PHYSICAL PLANNING	666257	128531	9110	114875	60710	313226		454229	72000	526229	839455	1505712	
	SAFE DRINKING WATER (Central Level)	105595	28531	1000	4789		34320		442800	62000	504800	539120	644715	
37.4.301	ADB – Third Phase Projects	79350						1165	250000	50000	300000	300000	379350	Asian Dev. Bank (ADB)
37.4.302	ADB – Fourth Phase Projects	14970							108000	12000	120000	120000	134970	Asian Dev. Bank (ADB)
37.4.310	Environm'l Sanitation Project	885		1000	3000		4000					4000	4885	UNICEF
37.4.320	National Information Management Projects	355			1789		1789					1789	2144	UNICEF
37.4.350	Manpower Dev. Project	2335	18531				18531					18531	20866	Asian Dev. Bank (ADB)
37.4.360	Drinking Water Quality Improvement Project	5000	5000				5000					5000	10000	Japan (DRE)
37.4.371	Bhaktapur Project		5000				5000					5000	5000	Germany
37.4.380	Rural Drinking Water and Sanitation Fund	2700							84800		84800	84800	87500	World Bank
	SAFE DRINKING WATER (District Level)	518591	100000	8110		60710	168820					168820	687411	
37.5.450	Rural Drinking Water Programme (undertaken by Dept, NGO and Rural Dev. Bank)	34135		3070		46930	50000					50000	84135	UNICEF
37.5.451	Rural Drinking Water (Western Region)	2956		200		5200	5400					5400	8356	Switzerland

Aid No.	Topic/Sub-topic	His Majesty's Government	Grant assistance					Loan				Total Assistance	Grand Total	Source of Aid
			Cash	To be paid	Direct payment	Materials	Total	Loan no.	To be paid	Direct payment	Total			
37.5.452	Tarai Tubewell Programme (undertaken by Dept, NGO Rural Development Bank)	2173		2850		7150	10000					10000	12173	UNICEF
37.5.460	Mechi Hill Dev. Programme (Drinking Water Project)	737		1990		1430	3420					3420	4157	Netherlands
37.5.470	District Level Drinking Water Section (Dept, NGO)	478590	100000				100000					100000	578590	Japan (DRF)
	HOUSING (Central level)	42071			110086		110086		11429	10000	21429	131515	173586	
37.4.625	Kathmandu Urban Area Dev. Project	42071						1240	11429	10000	21429	21429	63500	Asian Dev. Bank (ADF)
37.4.650	Committee for Municipality Development Fund	—			110086		110086					110086	110086	Germany
38.	MINISTRY OF INDUSTRY	1676			8408		8408		50380		50380	58788	60464	
38.4.260	Industrial Energy Management Project								50380		50380	50380	50380	World Bank
38.4.402	Rural Employment Projects	235			5160		5160					5160	5395	UNDP
38.4.403	Demographic Education Project	483			1848		1848					1848	2331	UNFPA
38.4.405	Seramics Project	958			1400		1400					1400	2358	Germany
40	MINISTRY OF AGRICULTURE	685821	452083	45367	150450		647900		259802	2800	262602	910502	1596323	
	CENTRAL LEVEL	413122	445650	24424	150450		620524		120894	2800	123694	744218	1157340	
40.4.210	Rural Development Marketing Project, Office of Coordinator (including Rukum)	2200		1804			1804					1804	4004	USA
40.4.250	Upper Everest Agriculture Development Project	4432							26419		26419	26419	30851	Asian Dev. Bank (ADB)
40.4.260	Assistant Crop Dev. Project	7350							58670	2800	61470	61470	68820	Asian Dev. Bank (ADB)
40.4.270	Agriculture Development Programme Janakpur	6200	32230				32230					32230	38530	Japan (K.R.2)
40.4.280	Silkworm Farming Development Project	2500	28252				28252					28252	30752	Japan (K.R.2)

Aid No.	Topic/Sub-topic	His Majesty's Government	Foreign Aid										Total Assistance	Grand Total	Source of Aid
			Grant assistance					Loan							
			Cash	To be paid	Direct payment	Materials	Total	Loan no.	To be paid	Direct payment	Total			
40.4.291	Horticulture Development Project, Kirtipur	2060	6612				6612					6612	8672	Japan (K.R.2)
40.4.380	Agriculture Training Programme (Centres)	5400	15025				15025					15025	20425	Japan (K.R.2)
40.4.400	Soil Test Service Programme	1875	5466				5466					5466	7341	Japan (K.R.2)
40.4.451	Small Markets Foundation Development Project	782			19985		19985					19985	20767	UN Capital Dev. Fund
40.4.541	Livestock Fertilisation and Care Project	610	12795				12795					12795	13405	German Counterpart Fund
40.4.550	Hill Bonded Forestry Project (Livestock development)	362							17338		17338	17338	17700	International Agricultural Dev. Fund
40.4.560	Veterinary Strengthen Project	612			130465		130465					130465	131077	European Community
40.5.570	Livestock Care Training Project	2500	8117				8117					8117	10617	Japan (K.R.2)
40.4.710	Agricultural Research Project	12640	24767				24767					24767	37407	Japan (K.R.2)
40.4.720	Agricultural Occupation and Technological System Project	46200		22620			22620					22620	68820	USA
40.4.730	Sub-crops Dev. Project	12749							18467		18467	18467	31216	Asian Dev. Bank (ADB)
40.4.750	National Watershed, Fisheries Development Project	4650	12286				12286					12286	16936	Japan (K.R.2)
40.4.800	Agricultural Materials Cost and Transportation Grant	300000	300000				300000					300000	600000	Germany
	DEPARTMENT OF AGRICULTURE (District Level)	153354	5717	11786			17503		83665		83665	101168	254522	
40.5.250	Upper Everest Agriculture Dev. Project	5509							4681		4681	4681	10190	Asian Dev. Bank (ADB)
40.5.260	Sub-crops Development Project	1349							8984		8984	8984	10333	Asian Dev. Bank (ADB)
40.5.410	Agriculture Transformation Programme	127600							70000		70000	70000	197600	World Bank
40.5.421	Mechi Hill Dev. Programme (Agriculture)		1227				1227					1227	1227	Netherlands
	RURAL DEV. MARKET PROJECT (Agriculture)	14406	11786	11786			11786					11786	26192	USA

Aid No.	Topic/Sub-topic	His Majesty's Government	Foreign Aid											Total Assistance	Grand Total	Source of Aid
			Grant assistance					Loan								
			Cash	To be paid	Direct payment	Materials	Total	Loan no.	To be paid	Direct payment	Total					
	DEPT. OF LIVESTOCK	119345	716	9157			9873		55243		55243			65116	184461	
40.5.511	Upper Everest Livestock Development Project	3984							5243		5243			5243	9227	Asian Dev. Bank (ADB)
40.5.512	Livestock Care Transformation Programme	104170							50000		50000			50000	154170	Asian Dev. Bank (ADB)
40.5.513	Mechi Hill Development Programme (Livestock)	-	716				716							716	716	Netherlands
40.5.580	Rural Dev. Market Project (Livestock)	11191		9157			9157							9157	20348	USA
46	MINISTRY OF POPULATION AND ENVIRONMENT	2376		11735			11735							11735	14111	UNPFA
46.4.200	National Population Programme	2376		11735			11735							11735	14111	
47	MINISTRY OF WATER RESOURCES	392307	74700	25500		110000	220200		1814038	439162	2253200			2473400	2865707	
	IRRIGATION	371405	72400			110000	182400		1814038	439162	2253200			2435600	2807005	
47.4.310	Irrigation Management Handover Project	103000						1311	45400	17400	62800			62800	73100	Asian Dev. Bank (ADB)
47.4.312	Irrigation Institutional Development Project	6500						1924/2044	51000	2500	53500			53500	60000	World Bank
47.4.313	First Irrigation Sector Project	15000						923	85000		85000			85000	100000	Asian Dev. Bank (ADB)
47.4.314	Second Irrigation Sector Project	51630						1437	320107	27393	347500			347500	399130	Asian Dev. Bank (ADB)
47.4.315	Irrigation Line of Credit	8000						1924/2144	211988	8012	220000			220000	228000	World Bank
47.4.340	River Control	44975				110000	110000							110000	154975	Japan
47.4.341	Watershed Disaster Control and Technical Centre	4185	50000				50000							50000	54185	Japan (K.R.2)
47.4.360	Bakralu River Control Project	5000							43300	1700	45000			45000	50000	OPEC Fund
47.4.361	Underground Water Investigation Programme	7075							2900	2100	5000			5000	12075	World Bank
47.4.401	Community Small Tube Irrigation Program	3700							36100	9900	46000			46000	49700	International Agri. Dev. Fund
47.4.401	Mechi Hill Irrigation Project		1500				1500							1500	1500	Netherlands

Aid No.	Topic/Sub-topic	His Majesty's Government	Foreign Aid										Total Assistance	Grand Total	Source of Aid
			Grant assistance					Loan							
			Cash	To be paid	Direct payment	Materials	Total	Loan no.	To be paid	Direct payment	Total				
47.4.402	Sunsari Morang Irrigation Project	31875							100000	30000	130000	130000	161875	World Bank
47.4.403	Chanda Mohana Irrigation Project	3500							26500		26500	26500	30000	OPEC Fund
47.4.404	Bagmali Irrigation Project	35970							195960	5940	201900	201900	237870	Southi Fund
47.4.405	Eastern Rapti Irrigation Project	36000						867	172000		172000	172000	208000	Asian Dev. Bank (ADB)
47.4.406	Bhairahawa–Lumbini Irrigation Project (III Phase)	29900						2144	265000	50000	315000	315000	344900	World Bank
47.4.407	Marchawar Irrigation Project (Second Stage)	8500	11400				11400					11400	19900	UNCDF
47.4.408	Dhawalagiri Zone Irrigation Project		9500				9500					9500	9500	ILO
47.4.410	Rajapur Irrigation Project	29820						1113	85783	164217	250000	250000	279820	Asian Dev. Bank (ADB)
47.4.411	Mahakali Irrigation Programme	29475						1924	173000	120000	293000	293000	332475	World Bank
	ELECTRICITY	20902	2300	35500			37800					37800	58702	
47.4.850	Local Interest in Electricity	500		35500			35500					35500	36000	USA
47.4.852	Multi-Purpose Project Study	20402	2300				2300					2300	22702	Japan, India
48	MINISTRY OF CONSTRUCTION & TRANSPORTATION	1302590	596500	42000	369618		1008118	9862	838981	1284287	2123268	3131386	4433976	
48.4.200	Mechi Highway (Phidim–Taplejung (including Kaveri))	10000	20000				20000					20000	30000	Japan (DRF)
48.4.201	Sagarmatha Highway (Gaighat–Diktel)	10000							10000		10000	10000	20000	Asian Dev. Bank (ADB)
48.4.202	Bnepe–Sinduli–Bardibas Road	7000			93000		93000					93000	100000	Japan
48.4.203	Rapti Highway (Salyan–Musikot)	9800							15000		15000	15000	24800	Asian Dev. Bank (ADB)
48.4.204	Karnali Highway (Surkhet–Jumla)	70000							30000		30000	30000	100000	Asian Dev. Bank (ADB)
48.4.205	Mahakali Highway, Baitadi–Darchula (including Chamelia Bridge)	19505	20000				20000		10000		10000	30000	49505	Japan / Asian Dev. Bank (ADB)

Aid No.	Topic/Sub-topic	His Majesty's Government	Foreign Aid										Grand Total	Source of Aid
			Grant assistance					Loan				Total Assistance		
			Cash	To be paid	Direct payment	Materials	Total	Loan no.	To be paid	Direct payment	Total			
48.4.252	Basantapur–Terathum–Aathrai Road	6000	4000				4000					4000	10000	Japan (DRF)
48.4.254	Basantapur–Chainpur–Khadbari Road	10000	5000				5000		5000		5000	10000	20000	Japan (DRF) 5000 Asian Dev. Bank 5000
48.4.255	Hile–Leguwaghat–Bhajpur Road	10000	5000				5000		5000		5000	10000	20000	Japan (DRF) 5000 Asian Dev. Bank 5000
48.4.256	Biratnagar–Rangeli Road		1000				1000					1000	1000	India
48.4.257	Chatara–Chakraghatti–Birpur		1000				1000					1000	1000	India
48.4.258	Katari Okhaldhunga	30000	10000				10000		10000		10000	20000	50000	Japan, Asian Dev. Bank
48.4.259	Bardibas–Jaleswar–Janakpur–Dhanusha	7350			40000		40000					40000	47350	UNCDF
48.4.262	Chhahare–Tokha	5000							5000		5000	5000	10000	Asian Dev. Bank
48.4.265	Dumre–Besisahar	19885						2347	130000		130000	130000	149885	World Bank
48.4.267	Rudravreni–Murtibung–Baglung–Dhorpatan (including Rudravreni Bridge)	10000	8000				8000					8000	18000	Japan (DRF)
48.4.268	Lumbini–Taulihawa–Tilaura Lot	10000	5000				5000					5000	15000	Japan (DRF)
48.4.270	Baglung–Beni–Jomsom	10000	10000				10000		5000		5000	15000	25000	Japan (DRF), ADB
48.4.272	Chhinju–Jajarkot	19950	10000				10000					10000	29950	Japan (DRF)
48.4.275	Khodpe–Bajang	30000	10000				10000			10000	10000	20000	50000	Japan, Asian Dev. Bank
48.4.276	Sahajpur–Dipayal	5000	5000				5000					5000	10000	Japan (DRF)
48.4.278	Sanphebagar–Mangalsen	10000							5000		5000	5000	15000	Asian Dev. Bank
48.4.280	Baitadi–Satbaj–Jhulaghat	7500							5000		5000	5000	12500	Asian Dev. Bank
48.4.299	Postman Roads	15000	10000				10000		10000		10000	20000	35000	Japan (DRF), ADB
48.4.501	Bisanmal Link Road (Kathmandu)	2000							18000		18000	18000	20000	Asian Dev. Bank
48.4.550	Road Maintenance and Rehabilitation Project	66300			16018		16018	2578	257891	386837	644728	660746	727046	World Bank, Switzerland
48.4.551	Road Maintenance Project	23000	100000				100000					100000	123000	England
48.4.552	Second Road Improvement Project	104842						982	80000	428000	508000	508000	612842	Asian Dev. Bank

Aid No.	Topic/Sub-topic	His Majesty's Government	Grant assistance					Loan				Total Assistance	Grand Total	Source of Aid
			Cash	To be paid	Direct payment	Materials	Total	Loan no.	To be paid	Direct payment	Total			
48.4.553	Third Road Improvement Project	74770						1377	93240	230000	323240	323240	398010	Asian Dev. Bank
48.4.554	Maintenance and Rehabilitation Co-ordination Unit	1500			9600		9600					9600	11100	England, Switzerland
48.4.555	Various Roads Maintenance and Construction Improvement	245000	65000				65000			50000	50000	115000	360000	Japan (DRF), ADB
48.4.554	Longer Road Rehabilitation Unit	9000			33000		33000					33000	42000	England
48.4.571	Sanasi-Imruwa-Kapurganj Road	5000	5000				5000					5000	10000	Japan (DRF)
48.4.575	Armiko Highway Rehabilitation Project	19825	83000				83000					83000	102825	Switzerland
48.4.576	Banepa-Panauice Road Strengthen Project	5000	8000				8000					8000	13000	France
48.4.577	Neubise-Malekhu-Muglina Maryangdi Road Project	17918						2578		82000	82000	82000	89918	World Bank
48.4.578	Malekhu-Dhading	1000	9000				9000					9000	10000	Germany
48.4.581	Goruinge-Sandhikharka	10000							7500		7500	7500	17500	Asian Dev. Bank
48.4.582	Chakchake-Libang	3000							2000		2000	2000	5000	Asian Dev. Bank
48.4.583	Nepalganj-Bagauda	3000							5000		5000	5000	8000	Asian Dev. Bank
48.4.690	Other Roads Construction and Rehabilitation	130000	60000				60000					60000	190000	Japan (DRF)
48.4.699	Various Roads Black Painting Programme	15000	30000				30000					30000	45000	Japan (DRF)
48.4.700	Suspension Bridges (Main Road)	34600		42000			42000					42000	76600	Switzerland
48.4.711	Sanasi Bridge (Baghorn Bridge, Bhaise-Hetanda Road)	10000			65000		65000					65000	75000	Germany
48.4.712	Seti Bridge (Kaski)	1000			19000		19000					19000	20000	China
48.4.713	Babai Bridge (Deng)	10000	5000				5000					5000	15000	Japan (DRF)
48.4.714	Kohalpur-Mahakali (22 bridges)	5965	94000		94000		94000					94000	99965	India
48.4.750	Bridge Construction Programme	42880	72500				72500		17800		17800	90300	133180	Japan (DRF) 72500, Asian Dev. Bank 17800
48.4.760	Bridges Conservation Programme	10000	10000				10000					10000	20000	Japan (DRF)

Aid No.	Topic/Sub-topic	His Majesty's Government	Foreign Aid									Total Assistance	Grand Total	Source of Aid
			Grant assistance					Loan						
			Cash	To be paid	Direct payment	Materials	Total	Loan no.	To be paid	Direct payment	Total			
48.4.800	Study and Design Survey of Potentiality of Bridges	20000							10000		10000	10000	30000	Asian Dev. Bank
48.4.854	Machine Repair		25000				25000					25000	25000	Japan (DRF)
48.4.855	Machinery Equipment Purchase	30000							50000		50000	50000	80000	Asian Dev. Bank
48.4.856	Kohalpur–Mahakali Claim (including ADB)	50000							50000		50000	50000	100000	Asian Dev. Bank
48.4.902	Nepal Multi-Model Transit and Trade Facilitation Project	20000							2550	97450	100000	100000	120000	World Bank
49	MINISTRY OF TOURISM AND CIVIL AVIATION	90261	49000		260000		309000		180436	168712	349148	658148	748409	
	TOURISM	12958							175436	28900	204336	204336	217234	
49.4.201	Tourism Base Dev. Project	11121							161999	27000	188999	188999	200120	Asian Dev. Bank
49.4.202	Second Tourism Base Dev. Project	1837							13437	1900	15337	15337	17174	Asian Dev. Bank
	AIRLINES	77303	49000		260000		309000		5000	139812	144812	453812	531115	
49.4.300	Tribhuwan International Airport Project	71813							5000	139812	144812	144812	216625	Asian Dev. Bank
49.4.303	Tribhuwan International Airport Modernization Project	5490			260000		260000					260000	265490	Japan
49.4.340	Life Relief and Fire Control Service		49000				49000					49000	49000	Japan (DRF)
55	MINISTRY OF LAND REFORM AND MANAGEMENT	2831			139397		139397					139397	142228	
55.4.310	Eastern Nepal Topographic Map Project	581			30000		30000					30000	30581	Finland
55.4.311	Western Nepal Topographic Map Project	2250			109397		109397					109397	111647	Finland
57	MINISTRY OF YOUTH, SPORTS AND CULTURE	80	49000		5500		54500					54500	54580	
57.4.520	Kahare Integrated Project		49000				49000					49000	49000	France
57.4.530	Kathmandu Valley Cultural Heritage Conservation Master Plan	80			5500		5500					5500	5580	Germany

Aid No.	Topic/Sub-topic	His Majesty's Government	Foreign Aid									Total Assistance	Grand Total	Source of Aid
			Grant assistance					Loan						
			Cash	To be paid	Direct payment	Materials	Total	Loan no.	To be paid	Direct payment	Total			
59	**MINISTRY OF FOREST AND SOIL CONSERVATION**	72435	51108	24231	75574	8180	159093		77331		77331	236424	308859	
	CENTRAL LEVEL	24550	21475	1985	20787		44247		47363		47363	91610	116160	
59.4.200	Forestry Research nand Survey Project	8370	971				971					971	9341	England
59.4.300	Environment and Forest Entrepreneur Programme			1985			1985					1985	1985	USA
59.4.311	Community Forest Dev. Programme	5757			5580		5580	2028	16950		16950	22530	28287	World Bank 16950 Denmark 5580
59.4.313	Hill Bonded Forest and Stage Dev. Project	446						250	30413		30413	30413	30859	Int. Agriculture Dev. Bank
59.4.330	Tree Improvement Programme	1965			15007		15007					15007	16972	Denmark
59.4.340	Chariya Forest Dev. Programme		2324				2324					2324	2324	Germany
59.4.350	Training and Communication Programme	4920	6830		200		7030					7030	11950	Japan (K.R.2) 6830 Denmark 200
59.4.610	Watershed Management Project	1479	1500				1500					1500	2979	Japan (K.R.2)
59.4.620	Basmati Watershed Project	1613	9850				9850					9850	11463	European Community
	DISTRICT LEVEL	47885	29833	22246	54787	8180	114846		29968		29968	144814	192699	
59.5.311	Community Forest Development Programme	5982			13833		13833	2028	29968		29968	43801	49783	World Bank 29968 Denmark 13833
59.5.401	Koshi–Dhawalagiri Rural Area Forest Development Project	15694	18330				18330					18330	34024	England
59.5.402	Dholakha–Ramechhap Community Forest Dev. Programme	5158			4239		4239					4239	9397	Switzerland
59.5.403	Sindhu Kabhre Forest Development Project	4955			5359		5359					5359	10314	Australia
59.5.410	Environment and Forest Industry Programme	50		15832			15632					15632	15682	USA
59.5.420	Mechi Hill Development Programme (Forest)		920				920					920	920	Netherlands
59.5.660	Mechi Hill Dev. Programme (Soil Conservation)		1674				1674					1674	1674	Netherlands

Aid No.	Topic/Sub-topic	His Majesty's Government	Foreign Aid									Total Assistance	Grand Total	Source of Aid
			Grant assistance					Loan						
			Cash	To be paid	Direct payment	Materials	Total	Loan no.	To be paid	Direct payment	Total			
59.5.661	Chure Soil and Watershed Conservation Project		2625				2625					2625	2625	Germany
59.5.662	Sindhu Kabhre Soil Conservation Project	1249			2416		2416					2416	3665	Australia
59.5.663	Watershed Management Project (Rasuwa, Nuwakot Dhadng)	3234			12640		12640					12640	15874	Denmark
59.5.664	Begnas Rupatal Programme	859	565			2325	2890					2890	3749	Care/Nepal
59.5.665	Upper Adhikhola Watershed Management Project	1718	1259			5855	7114					7114	8832	Care/Nepal
59.5.670	Environment and Forest Industry Programme (Soil Conserv.)	7976		5384			5384					5384	13360	USA
59.5.680	Community Development and Forest/Watershed Project	1010	4260		16300		20560					20560	21570	Japan (K.R.2)
59.5.750	Environment and Forest Industrial Programme (Wildlife)			1230			1230					1230	1230	USA
65	MINISTRY OF EDUCATION	445574	273092	62988	39148	300099	675327		1070548	296519	1367067	2042394	2487968	
	CENTRAL LEVEL	383471	165959	62988	39148	180099	388194		759637	296519	1056156	1444350	1827821	
65.4.410	Basic and Primary Education Project	8885	64937				64937	2357	64095	16000	80095	145032	153917	World Bank 80095 Unicef 12838 Denmark 52099
65.4.420	Primary Education Dev. Project	38062						1141	313590		313590	313590	351672	Asian Dev. Bank
65.4.430	Secondary Education Dev. Project	30466						1196	102315	60000	162315	162315	192781	Asian Dev. Bank
65.4.450	Council for Technical/Vocational Education (CTEVT)	17998	3448			700	4148	974 Nep.	133799		133799	137947	155945	Switzerland, ADB
65.4.451	Technical Institutes	33344	3951			3540	7491	974 Nep.	13889		13889	21380	54724	Switzerland, ADB
65.4.453	Pokhara Tourism Training Centre	618								1407	1407	1407	2025	Asian Dev. Bank
65.4.460	Tribhuwan University Central Office	43813						2044 Nep.	114070	50000	164070	164070	207883	World Bank
65.4.461	Institute of Engineering	38170		58792	39148		97940	2044 Nep.	17879	169112	186991	284931	323101	Switzerland, World Bank
65.4.462	Institute of Medicine	34761	9490				9490					9490	44251	Redd Barna, WHO, Canada, Denmark

Aid No.	Topic/Sub-topic	His Majesty's Government	Foreign Aid										Grand Total	Source of Aid
			Grant assistance					Loan				Total Assistance		
			Cash	To be paid	Direct payment	Materials	Total	Loan no.	To be paid	Direct payment	Total			
65.4.463	Institute of Agriculture	5499		1900			1900					1900	7399	USA
65.4.465	Institute of Science and Technology	3500	1525				1525					1525	5025	USA
65.4.600	Non-Formal Education	90000		2296			2296					2296	92296	UNFPA
65.4.620	Primary School Dietary Prog.	14835				175855	175859					175859	190694	W.F.O.
65.4.630	Demographic Education		11108				11108					11108	11108	UNFPA
65.4.670	Nepal National Secretariat for UNESCO	1500	1500				1500					1500	3000	UNICEF
65.4.680	RONAST	22000	10000				10000					10000	32000	Germany (Ka. Pa. fm)
	District Level	62103	154133			120000	287133		310911		310911	598044	660147	
65.5.410	Basic and Primary Education Project	62103	167133			120000	287133		310911		310911	598044	660147	World Bank, Japan (B) UNICEF, Denmark
67	MINISTRY OF INFORMATION AND COMMUNICATION	1150	10000	8000			18000					18000	19150	
67.4.300	Secured Printing Project	1150	10000				10000					10000	10000	France
67.4.450	Telecommunication Sector Reform Project	1150		8000			8000					8000	9150	Denmark
69	MINISTRY OF LOCAL DEVELOPMENT	436485	57394	117158	114500	116300	405352		165416	30100	195516	600862	103753	
	CENTRAL LEVEL	8070	4286	2297			6583		23203	100	23303	29886	37956	
69.4.200	Women's Dev. Programme	3399		2297			2297	208-1237	17126		17126	19423	22822	World Bank, UNFPA, IFFD
69.4.230	Demographic Education Programme	350	2786				2786					2786	3136	UN Population Fund
69.4.260	Flood Area Reconstruction and Rehabilitation Project	116						352	4147		4147	4147	4263	Int. Agriculture Dev. Bank
69.4.290	Rural Baseline Development Programme	205						1450	430	100	530	530	735	Asian Dev. Bank
69.4.300	Lumbini Zone Rural drinking Water and Sanitation Project	1500	1500				1500					1500	3000	Finland
69.4.320	Institute for National Ethnic Groups Upliftment	2500					1500		1500		1500	1500	4000	Asian Development Bank

Aid No.	Topic/Sub-topic	His Majesty's Government	Foreign Aid										Total Assistance	Grand Total	Source of Aid
			Grant assistance					Loan							
			Cash	To be paid	Direct payment	Materials	Total	Loan no.	To be paid	Direct payment	Total			
	DISTRICT LEVEL	428415	53108	114861	114500	116300	358769		142213	30000	172213	570982	999397	
69.5.200	Women's Dev. Programme	34059		16261			16261	208-1237	37195		37195	53456	877515	IFPD, ADB, USA, UNICEF, Japan, UNFPA
69.5.210	Remote Area Dev. Programme	54900				20100	20100					20100	75000	Care/Nepal
69.5.260	Flood Area Reconstruction and Rehabilitation Project	521						352	1318		1318	1318	1839	Int. Agriculture Dev. Bank
69.5.280	Rural Community Baseline Development Programme	80645	12500			93150	105650					105650	186295	World Food Programme
69.5.290	Rural Baseline Dev. Programme	13115						1450	33750		33750	33750	46865	Asian Dev. Bank
69.5.300	Lumbini Zone Rural Drinking Water and Sanitation Project	15680	15680				15680					15680	31360	Finland
69.5.400	Solid Waste Management Programme (Ubhapurwa Road Gokarna Laddick)	97000			110000		110000					110000	207000	Germany
69.5.410	Remote Portable Road Reconstruction Project	5310						2578	69950	30000	99950	99950	105260	World Bank
69.5.451	Dhading I.R.D. Project	470	6878				6878					6878	7348	Germany
69.5.452	Galmi I.R.D. Project (IRDP)	700		49300			49300					49300	50000	European Community
69.5.453	Arghakhachi IRDP	700		49300			49300					49300	50000	European Community
69.5.454	Gorkha Development Project	165	14300				14300					14300	14456	Germany
69.5.455	Lamjung Development Project	150	3750				3750					3750	3900	Germany
69.5.456	Palm Conservation and Development Programme				4500		4500					4500	4500	Germany
	LOCAL DEVELOPMENT CONSTRUCTION PROGRAMME	125000				3050	3050					3050	128050	World Food Programme
70	MINISTRY OF HEALTH	402268	196028	46602	242990	278336	763956		505941	39484	545425	1309381	1711649	
	CENTRAL LEVEL PROJECTS	227304	108516	8587		272913	390016		471767	39484	511251	901267	1128571	
70.4.306	B.P. Koirala Memorial Cancer Hospital	1000			80000		80000					80000	81000	China
70.4.321	Martyr Gangalal Cardiac Disease Treatment Centre – Maharajganj	5000	10000				10000					10000	15000	Adra

Aid No.	Topic/Sub-topic	His Majesty's Government	Grant assistance					Loan				Total Assistance	Grand Total	Source of Aid
			Cash	To be paid	Direct payment	Materials	Total	Loan no.	To be paid	Direct payment	Total			
70.4.330	B.P. Koirala Medical Science Institute	250000			404300		404300					404300	654300	India
70.4.403	Goitre Control Project	10000	47080				47080					47080	57080	India
70.4.450	Population and Family Health Project	52617						2600	467206	39484	506690	506690	559307	World Bank
70.4.451	Nepal Family Planning and MCH Programme	2969	1376	540			1916					1916	4885	UNFPA USA
70.4.453	Integrated Supervision	105							945		945	945	1050	World Bank
70.4.454	Lady Health Volunteer (CHV)	370				6500	6500					6500	6870	UNICEF, UNFPA
70.4.470	EPI Programme (Immunization)	31827				44790	44790					44790	76617	UNICEF
70.4.471	National Polio Vaccination Prog.	5000				40000	40000					40000	45000	Rotary Int..., USA, C.D.C.
70.4.474	Nutrition Programme	4150	450			39550	40000					40000	44150	UNICEF, USA
70.4.511	Malaria/Kalajwar Control Prog.	49725	21307				21307					21307	71032	Japan (DRF)
70.4.512	Leprosy Control Programme	1238	522				522					522	1760	N.S.L., I.N.F.
70.4.710	Medicine and Medical Equipments Supply	47079	15000			141237	156237		1890		1890	158127	205206	Germany, Japan (DRF) World Bank, Japan
70.4.740	Management Information System	2000	6000				6000					6000	8000	Germany (Ka. Pa. fm)
70.4.750	National Health Education Information Centre	9000	9796	3620		282	13698					13698	22698	UNFPA, USA, WHO
70.4.760	National Training Programme	9299	4795	4427		554	9776				1726	11502	20801	UNFPA, USA, World Bank, Redd Barna
70.4.780	Pathology Service	1925	2190				2190					2190	4115	WHO
70.4.920	Other Miscellaneous (Homeopathic Service)	26012	400				400					400	26412	WHO
	DISTRICT-WIDE PROJECTS	33958	82312	38015	840	5423	126590		34174		34174	160764	194722	
70.4.451	Nepal Family Planning & MCH Programme	23282	18991	19704		5423	44118					44118	67400	UNFPA, UNDP
70.5.453	Integrated Supervision	1711							34174		34174	34174	35885	World Bank
70.5.454	Lady Health Volunteer (CHV)	53	5516	1820			7336					7336	7389	UNFPA, USA, UNICEF
70.5.472	Diarrhoeal Diseases Control Prog.		523	523			523					523	523	USA

Aid No.	Topic/Sub-topic	His Majesty's Government	Grant: Cash	Grant: To be paid	Grant: Direct payment	Grant: Materials	Grant: Total	Loan no.	Loan: To be paid	Loan: Direct payment	Loan: Total	Total Assistance	Grand Total	Source of Aid
70.5.474	Nutrition Programme		865				865					865	865	USA
70.5.512	Leprosy Control Programme	500			840		840					840	1340	I.N.F., N.L.S.
70.5.750	National Health Education Information and Communication	1425	7203				7203					7203	8628	UNFPA
70.5.760	National Training Programme	6987	49737	15968			65705					65705	72692	UNFPA, UNICEF, USA, Redd Barna, Eur. Comm.
71	MINISTRY OF LABOUR		1159				1159					1159	1159	
71.4.300	Informal Sector Demographic Education Programme		1159				1159					1159	1159	UN Population Fund
72	SECRETARIAT OF THE NATIONAL PLANNING COMMISSION	2781			12500		12500					12500	15281	
72.4.350	Nepal Life Standard Measurement Survey	2781			12500		12500					12500	15281	World Bank
87	MINISTRY OF FINANCE–INVESTMENT	494520	55000	30000	1187970		1272970		1094270	5011253	610523	7378493	7873013	
	BANKING SECTOR	85000	20000	30000			50000		537000		537000	587000	672000	
87.4.201	Agriculture Dev. Bank (share investment)	85000	20000				20000					20000	105000	Germany
87.4.202	Small Farmers Development Programme – III Phase								500000		500000	500000	500000	Asian Dev. Bank
87.4.203	Production Loan Programme for Rural Women's Development								15000		15000	15000	15000	Int. Agriculture Dev. Bank
87.4.204	Hill Bonded Forest and Stage Development Programme								15000		15000	15000	15000	Int. Agriculture Dev. Bank
87.4.210	Gulmi–Arghakhachi IRDP			30000			30000					30000	30000	European Community
87.4.251	Underground Irrigation and Flood Rehabilitation Programme								7000		7000	7000	7000	Int. Agriculture Dev. Bank
	MINISTRY OF SUPPLIES								354770	97363	452133	452133	452133	
87.4.301	Nepal Oil Corporation							987	354770	97363	452133	452133	452133	Asian Dev. Bank
	DRINKING WATER	105000							142500	350000	492500	492500	597500	

Aid No.	Topic/Sub-topic	His Majesty's Government	Grant assistance (Foreign Aid)					Loan (Foreign Aid)				Total Assistance	Grand Total	Source of Aid
			Cash	To be paid	Direct payment	Materials	Total	Loan no.	To be paid	Direct payment	Total			
87.4.450	Urban Area Drinking Water and Sanitation Rehabilitation Prog.	70000							100000	350000	450000	450000	520000	World Bank
87.4.452	Drinking Water Production Improvement Programme	10000							32500		32500	32500	42500	Asian Dev. Bank
87.4.455	Drinking Water and Waste Management Programme	25000							10000		10000	10000	35000	Asian Dev. Bank
	ELECTRICITY	304520	35000		937970		972970		60000	4063890	4123890	5096860	5401380	
87.4.601	Kaligandaki (A) Water Dev. Project	159980								1505650	1505650	1505650	1665630	Asian Dev. Bank
87.4.602	Modikhola Water Dev. Project	1000								219000	219000	219000	220000	Korea
37.4.608	Ilam–Puwakhola	31310	30000				30000					30000	61310	Japan (DRF)
87.4.609	Dahabi Multifuel Extension Programme	4770								600000	600000	600000	604770	Finland, Nordic Fund
87.4.650	Dahabi–Bharatabari Proposed Ext. 132 KV							2347		3000	3000	3000	3000	World Bank
87.4.652	Khimti–Bhaktapur–Balaju 132 KV	7320			70000		70000					70000	77320	Finland
87.4.653	Devighat–Dhading 33 KV	5000			20000		20000					20000	25000	Germany
87.4.656	Siduwa–Khadbari 33 KV	1000			1000		1000					1000	2000	Germany
87.4.700	7th Electricity Project	40000						1011	60000	740000	800000	800000	840000	Asian Dev. Bank
87.4.710	Damre–Besisahar Rural Dev. Project	1110						37		7200	7200	7200	8310	Nordic Fund
87.4.724	Trisuli–Devighat Hydroelectricity Project	4350						2347		74520	74520	74520	78870	W. Bank
87.4.730	Small Hydroelectricity Project Master Plan	4200	5000				5000					5000	9200	Germany
87.4.740	Medium Size Hydroelectricity Project	3500						2347		119700	119700	119700	123200	World Bank
87.4.750	Valley Distribution System Strengthening	3750			750000		750000					750000	753750	Japan
87.4.752	High Voltage Save Tickets	540						37		48150	48150	48150	48690	Nordic Fund
87.4.753	High Voltage Improvement Programme	16980						2347		119250	119250	119250	136230	World Bank

Aid No.	Topic/Sub-topic	His Majesty's Government	Grant assistance					Loan				Total Assist-ance	Grand Total	Source of Aid
			Cash	To be paid	Direct payment	Materials	Total	Loan no.	To be paid	Direct payment	Total			
87.4.754	Gravity Supply Centre Extension Programme	150			5000		5000	SEF-2				5000	5150	Germany
87.4.810	Central workshop construction	2970						2347		20000	20000	20000	22970	World Bank
87.4.811	Physical Facilities of NEA	450						2347		9810	9810	9810	10260	World Bank
87.4.812	Training Facility							2347		50000	50000	50000	50000	World Bank
87.4.813	Computerised Billing							2347		5000	5000	5000	5000	World Bank
87.4.814	Computerised Account							2347		2000	2000	2000	2000	World Bank
87.4.815	Store Management							2347		3000	3000	3000	3000	World Bank
87.4.816	Electricity Linkage Control									61110	61110	61110	61110	Asian Dev. Bank
87.4.820	Kulekhani Conser. Project (II)	13500								472500	472500	472500	486000	Japan (OKCF)
87.4.830	Marsyangdi Electricity Centre	2340			70000		70000					70000	72340	Germany
87.4.840	Environmental Section Improvement				20970		20970					20970	20970	Asian Dev. Bank
87.4.850	NEA Commercialization									1000	1000	1000	1000	Asian Dev. Bank
87.4.860	Electrical System Master Plan									3000	3000	3000	3000	Asian Dev. Bank
87.4.951	COMMUNICATION				250000			87		500000					
87.4.951	Nepal Telecommunication Corporation				250000		250000	87		500000	500000	750000	750000	World Bank, Japan, Denmark
88	MINISTRY OF FINANCE (INVEST.)								92817		92817	92817	92817	Asian Dev. Bank
88.4.201	Kathmandu Urban Area Dev. Programme (Investment)								92817		92817	92817	92817	Asian Dev. Bank

The Nordic Institute of Asian Studies (NIAS) is funded by the governments of Denmark, Finland, Iceland, Norway and Sweden via the Nordic Council of Ministers, and works to encourage and support Asian studies in the Nordic countries. In so doing, NIAS has published well in excess of one hundred books in the last three decades, most of them in co-operation with Curzon Press.

Nordic Council of Ministers

For Product Safety Concerns and Information please contact our EU
representative GPSR@taylorandfrancis.com
Taylor & Francis Verlag GmbH, Kaufingerstraße 24, 80331 München, Germany

www.ingramcontent.com/pod-product-compliance
Ingram Content Group UK Ltd.
Pitfield, Milton Keynes, MK11 3LW, UK
UKHW042200240425
457818UK00011B/314